OWN YOUR GREATNESS

OWN YOUR GREATNESS

Overcome IMPOSTOR SYNDROME, Beat Self-Doubt, and Succeed in Life

**Lisa Orbé-Austin, PhD
and Richard Orbé-Austin, PhD**

ULYSSES PRESS

Published by:
Ulysses Press
P.O. Box 3440
Berkeley, CA 94703
www.ulyssespress.com

ISBN: 978-1-64604-024-7
Library of Congress Catalog Number: 2019951366

Printed in the United States by Kingery Printing Company
10 9 8 7 6 5 4 3 2

Acquisitions editor: Bridget Thoreson
Managing editor: Claire Chun
Editor: Renee Rutledge
Proofreader: Kate St.Clair
Cover design: Ashley Prine
Cover and interior art: © Vandathai/shutterstock.com
Interior design and production: Jake Flaherty

IMPORTANT NOTE TO READERS: This book has been written and published for informational and educational purposes only. It is not intended to serve as medical advice or to be any form of medical treatment. You should always consult with your physician before altering or changing any aspect of your medical treatment. Do not stop or change any prescription medications without the guidance and advice of your physician. Any use of the information in this book is made on the reader's good judgment and is the reader's sole responsibility. This book is not intended to diagnose or treat any medical condition and is not a substitute for a physician. This book is independently authored and published, and no sponsorship or endorsement of this book by, and no affiliation with, any trademarked brands or other products mentioned within is claimed or suggested. All trademarks that appear in this book belong to their respective owners and are used here for informational purposes only. The author and publisher encourage readers to patronize the quality brands mentioned in this book.

CONTENTS

INTRODUCTION

I was paralyzed, unable to make a move. I was stuck in a job that was far beneath my skill sets, underpaid, and treated poorly. I had all the credentials to take a leap—a PhD from an Ivy League university, two master's degrees, and connections in the right places—but I was terrified and doubted the power of any of it. I was fearful that if I left, my boss might try to bad-mouth me, which would ruin all the goodwill that I had built around those relationships. I was fearful about my ability to do anything else beyond this job. I was fearful about almost everything related to leaving this job, so I stayed.

—Lisa Orbé-Austin

That's what impostor syndrome can do to you. We know the feeling, because we have lived it. It can render your credentials worthless to your advancement, to earnings, to having agency in your life. It can soak you in fear so badly that you dismiss any other feelings that encourage you to leave, take a risk, or pursue an unknown opportunity. Being plagued by the thought that you will be found out as a fraud can leave you stuck at places for a sense of security—security that will never come from that outside place or person. The real security will come from facing your impostor syndrome, using the tools that we will equip you with in this book to combat it, and finally, owning your greatness.

We believe that owning your greatness means giving less power to your impostor syndrome and being able to consistently have more confidence in your abilities to succeed in life.

This workbook represents years of work supported by 40 years of research as well as our own observations, analyses, and lived experiences to develop a method to eradicate the impact of impostor syndrome in amazing, successful, and powerful people who existed for years believing that none of that was true. We hope that you will really engage with this book—write in it, dog-ear pages, highlight, put notes in the margins, staple notes to the book. It is meant to be used and used well. It's not meant to be kept in pristine condition. We know that perfectionism is a very central component of impostor syndrome, but we want you to work on it from the very start of engaging this book and the endeavor that you are undertaking to confront your impostor syndrome head on.

Throughout the book, hypothetical case studies are provided for illustrative purposes only and do not represent an actual client or an actual client's experience, but rather are meant to provide an example of the process and methodology of the book. An individual's experience may vary based on his or her individual circumstances. There can be no assurance that everyone will be able to achieve similar results in comparable situations. No portion of this book is to be interpreted as a testimonial or endorsement of our services.

Chapter 1

AN OVERVIEW AND ASSESSMENT OF IMPOSTOR SYNDROME

In the 1970s, two psychologists, Pauline R. Clance and Suzanne A. Imes, were working in the college counseling center at Georgia State University when they first observed this phenomenon in the women that they were treating. Drs. Clance and Imes noticed that they were working with very outwardly accomplished women, both students and faculty, who felt that they had acquired these credentials and opportunities in a fraudulent manner, and that at any moment they could be found out. They wrote a paper in 1978,[1] coining the term "impostor phenomenon." The paper outlined the characteristics of this syndrome, presented their first observations on the interventions that worked best to eradicate it, and listed the factors contributing to its development.

Impostor syndrome is the experience of constantly feeling like a fraud, downplaying one's accomplishments, and always being concerned about being exposed as incompetent or incapable. As a result, people with impostor syndrome engage in either overworking or self-sabotage. Impostor syndrome affects high-achieving professionals who are seemingly successful. However, when experiencing impostor syndrome, you are unable to enjoy your success and believe that this success is precarious. Research indicates that 70 percent of all people have experienced the Impostor Phenomenon at some point in their lives.[2] Impostor

---

1   Clance and Imes, "The Impostor Phenomenon in High-Achieving Women," 241–47.

2   Gravois, "You're Not Fooling Anyone," in *If I'm So Successful, Why Do I Feel Like a Fake?* eds. Joan C. Harvey and Cynthia Katz (New York: Random House, 1985).

syndrome is not a diagnostic classification but rather a group of thoughts, behaviors, and feelings that cluster together to create this syndrome and have a significant impact on your emotional functioning. This syndrome can feed feelings of anxiety, low self-esteem, depression, and frustration due to the thoughts and behaviors that result.[3]

SIGNS OF IMPOSTOR SYNDROME

Here are the signs that you may be struggling with impostor syndrome.

- You are high achieving.

- You engage in The Impostor Cycle (see page 5).

- You desire to be "special" or "the best."

- You deny ability and attribute success to luck, mistake, overwork, or a result of a relationship.

- You discount praise, feeling fear and guilt about success.

- You fear failure and being discovered as a fraud.

- You do not feel intelligent.

- You have anxiety, self-esteem issues, depression, and frustration from internal standards.

- You struggle with perfectionism.

- You overestimate others and underestimate oneself.

- You do not experience an internal feeling of success.

- You overwork or self-sabotage to cover the feelings of inadequacy.

Initially, Clance and Imes thought that impostor phenomenon would be found predominantly in women because of societal stereotyping that leads women to feel that they are less competent in certain domains (e.g., math, science, leadership). However, the research has been inconsistent and often finds that it is represented equally in men and women, although the findings suggest that women and men with impostor syndrome may behave differently in response to it.[4] It seems that men may be more prone to avoid situations where they might be exposed as a fraud and tend to compare themselves to peers with fewer qualifications. This allows them a protective mechanism that buoys their self-esteem, although it also leaves

---

3   Cozzarelli and Major, "Exploring the Validity of the Impostor Phenomenon," 401–17; McGregor, Gee, and Posey, "I Feel Like a Fraud," 43–48.
4   Cromwell et al., "The Impostor Phenomenon and Personality Characteristics," 563–67; Bernard et al., "Applying the Big Five Personality Factors," 321–33.

them underachieving.[5] Women with impostor syndrome, on the other hand, choose to remain in situations where they are constantly plagued by the fraudulent feelings.[6] We will explore these differences further in Gender Differences on page 11.

IMPACT ON EDUCATION AND CAREER

Clance and Imes noted that there were four particular hallmarks of impostor syndrome in the women they studied: 1) diligence and hard work; 2) intellectual inauthenticity; 3) charm and perceptiveness; 4) seeking mentorship for the purpose of external validation.

1. DILIGENCE AND HARD WORK

In their seminal paper, Clance and Imes found that the women that they had observed used hard work and diligence as a cover-up for their perceived inadequacy. The women would engage in a cycle that looked like:

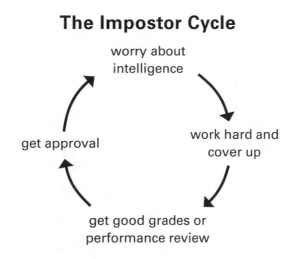

The Impostor Cycle

worry about intelligence

work hard and cover up

get good grades or performance review

get approval

Receiving the praise would result in temporarily feeling good and at that point, once the good feelings subsided, they returned again to worrying about intelligence or ability to perform. Within this cycle, there is no internalization of the successful experience. The accomplishment isn't accepted as part of their identity or attributed much value, so the next time they perform, it's as if the previous accomplishments never existed. Thus, the cycle begins again. In more recent research, it has been revealed that people do not only engage in hard work in that

---

5   Chayer and Bouffard, "Relations between Impostor Feelings and Upward and Downward Identification," 125–40.

6   Tao and Gloria, "Should I Stay or Should I Go?" 1–14.

second stage but can go in the opposite direction with self-sabotage. This is most commonly seen when someone with impostor syndrome procrastinates, usually due to anxiety about performance and perfectionism, as they attempt to unveil themselves as an impostor.[7] The belief is that the procrastination serves as a method to expose their status as an impostor, perhaps in hopes of releasing the stress and strain of it. However, they usually still perform well. But any mistake is interpreted as proof of their inadequacy due to their perfectionism, rather than as an artifact of being human, or of not giving themselves enough time to review the work.

The experience of self-sabotage can sometimes be hard to detect as it's often connected to the performance anxiety, and this anxiety makes it difficult to tease out what has occurred. It can be seen in spontaneous and impulsive decisions to go against a plan, trouble organizing for high-stress events, or other subtle behaviors that affect preparedness, confidence, and performance.

In this example of Brenda, a school teacher, you will see how tiny choices influenced by anxiety serve to reinforce the performance issues and the impostor experiences:

Brenda is a fourth-grade math teacher who sought counseling due to her unhappiness with her current job of five years. She wants to explore other job options. In fact, she dreads going to work every day.

During our first session, Brenda was very tearful about her dissatisfaction but believed that she did not have many options. Although she has received countless positive performance reviews, Brenda did not regard herself as a good teacher. Rather, she thought that because she was so good-natured, people really liked her and gave her positive scores on her performance reviews.

As our work progressed, we were able to identify Brenda's impostor syndrome and her self-sabotage tendencies that result from it. For instance, on the day of her teacher observation, Brenda covered a different lesson, one that should have been taught in three weeks, rather than the one she had prepared for the observation. As might be expected, the students were a bit lost and were not able to keep up. Brenda was certain that her observation went poorly and she would finally be revealed as an unskilled and incompetent teacher. However, the teacher who conducted her

---

7   Chayer and Bouffard, "Relations between Impostor Feelings and Upward and Downward Identification," 125–40; Yuen and Depper, "Fear of Failure in Women," 21–39.

observation was highly impressed with Brenda's poise and her ability to engage her students despite the material being a bit advanced. She gave Brenda a positive review.

In another instance, Brenda had to call in sick on the day of her interview for another role. The school where she was to interview, however, wanted to meet her so badly that they immediately rescheduled her interview based on her availability. Brenda went on the interview and was offered the role. Unfortunately, she turned it down, because she did not yet feel ready to leave.

2. INTELLECTUAL INAUTHENTICITY

The second characteristic of impostor syndrome that Clance and Imes illustrated is intellectual inauthenticity, or the downplaying of knowledge, skills, or abilities, or not revealing true opinions of a situation in order to protect someone else's feelings or preserve the relationship. When someone with impostor syndrome behaves like this, it only furthers their belief that they have engaged in some form of deception, exacerbating the feelings of being fraudulent. The kind of relationships that this intellectual inauthenticity might preserve are those with people who demonstrate narcissistic characteristics (e.g., needing excessive praise and not being able to tolerate critique or dissent) and/or have a fragile sense of themselves and their accomplishments. These can be dangerous people for those with impostor syndrome to connect with. You can see this as illustrated in Elise's ongoing experience at the company where she has been a longtime employee:

Elise has been an office administrator at the same institution for 25 years. She has watched leaders come and go and has a significant level of understanding of the company's history as well as an unusual expertise in the subject matter, for her position, because she has been so intimately involved in the company's evolution. Every time another CEO is hired—and there have been many—she struggles to share her content and cultural knowledge because she senses their fragility and notices their desire to be the most knowledgeable person in the room, even though they are brand-new. In each experience with a new CEO, she becomes terrified that she will be fired because she will be seen as incompetent and outdated in her knowledge and skills.

3. CHARM AND PERCEPTIVENESS

Intellectual inauthenticity is often combined with a third behavior, which is utilizing charm and perceptiveness. In their ability to get people to like them and potentially advocate for them, those with impostor syndrome can feel like their ability to fool people extends beyond their intellectual capacity.

People with impostor syndrome can also exhibit high emotional intelligence. They are particularly keen at understanding what others need to make them feel valued and connected to them. They may utilize these skills, especially with mentors and senior leaders to generate positive evaluations of their behavior. However, a mentor who is not benevolent, and perhaps narcissistic as mentioned earlier, may exploit their yearning for connection and praise to maximize their performance. The potential for a truly dysfunctional relationship is highly likely in these cases. The person with impostor syndrome can find themselves in a situation where the mentor or supervisor makes them feel like they ARE truly an impostor and must constantly and unendingly prove themselves. These types of relationships become very hard to break because the person with impostor syndrome may feel as if their ineptitude has been found out, so they continually seek some sort of validation from someone who will never or very rarely provide it, because it keeps the person with impostor syndrome working hard for them.

4. SEEKING MENTORSHIP FOR THE PURPOSE OF EXTERNAL VALIDATION

The final behavior that maintains the impostor syndrome is seeking a mentoring relationship from someone, who is well respected in their field, industry, school, or office, in order to gain external validation. But this relationship may be fraught for the person with impostor syndrome for the reason discussed above, or because it can feel inauthentic if the person with impostor syndrome believes they charmed the mentor into positive feedback because they think it has been acquired through duplicitous means (e.g., through charm).

In this example, Sam believes that his positive relationship with mentors and senior leaders has caused them to promote him unjustly, which creates fear and discomfort with his new role:

Sam just got his 3rd promotion at a technology start-up where he has been working since almost right out of college. He's terrified about the new role and feels he is out of his depth. Everyone at his new level is at least 10 years older than him and have been at big impressive tech giants. Sam is convinced that he is sitting in this seat because he is just very good at getting along with his bosses. He feels like he may have accidentally convinced them simply with his social acumen that he can take on these new roles. In spite of consistent glowing performance reviews from different supervisors, which he believes are inflated, he is terrified of falling on his face in this new job.

In addition, it has been shown that people struggling with impostor syndrome have lower levels of job and career satisfaction, yet higher levels of organizational commitment. So, while people with impostor syndrome tend to be more unhappy in their jobs and careers, they are also likely to commit to these places that are making them unhappy, perhaps in an effort to create some sense of stability and predictability in terms of evaluation. Further, the research also indicates that people with impostor syndrome struggle with marketing themselves, which is critical for job searching or networking. Therefore, their salaries and promotions are usually negatively impacted, which can be seen in lower salaries and fewer promotions. It also shows up in being less optimistic about their career and being less adaptable when things go wrong. Moreover, those with impostor syndrome are likely to have a reduced knowledge of the job market, which makes taking a leap to a new role when they are unhappy even more difficult.

Throughout our experience working with impostor syndrome, we have seen it show up in the following ways that affect professional development:

- Not understanding their worth (i.e., salary comps) in the marketplace
- Fear of negotiating
- Lack of motivation to leave stagnating roles
- Reluctance to vie for promotion
- Avoidance of high-visibility stretch assignments
- Difficulty networking and communicating their accomplishments to others
- Trouble envisioning their long-term career future

All of these behaviors of impostor syndrome have a significant impact on advancement, salary, and long-term earnings, but they can be reversed.

THE PROFESSIONAL IMPACT OF
YOUR IMPOSTOR SYNDROME

What behaviors related to your impostor syndrome do you find yourself exhibiting? Give a concrete example of each to ground your response in an actual instance. List the behaviors and examples here:

_____

_____

_____

_____

_____

TRAIT VS. STATE

People with impostor syndrome consistently ask, "Is this inherently who I am? Part of my character? Or can I really change this?" Impostor syndrome does not appear to be characterological (i.e., part of your personality) or a trait. It seems that there are certain experiences in family dynamics, beliefs about yourself, and roles that you tend to play that make it more likely for you to have the propensity to struggle with impostor syndrome. In other words, you were not born like this no matter what other people tell you or want you to believe.

You may struggle to let go of certain behaviors, thoughts, and feelings connected to impostor syndrome because of the belief that your current success or accomplishments are a result of these behaviors, and if you let them go, all will be lost. Behaviors such as overworking and perfectionism are the hardest to change—largely, we believe, because they are reinforced in our environments. Today, it is very easy to "log back on" to your company's systems when you go home and work inordinately long hours. If you do more work, get more done, push ahead of deadlines, certainly no one at work is going to reprimand you or tell you to work less, and you are likely going to get the praise you are seeking for being a good, worthy employee. However, it is exactly this behavior that reinforces the impostor syndrome and the ideas that you are not naturally talented and therefore, must give more to be on par with everyone else. Hearing that "mistakes are costly" and seeing colleagues and others around you criticized when they make an error also supports perfectionism. These behaviors can also feed on each other. When people are perfectionistic, they often struggle to delegate tasks and manage down well (i.e., manage direct reports or junior colleagues) because they are concerned about how their colleagues' work product will reflect on them. Thus, they often overwork, doing their job as well as a ton of other people's jobs, which often leads to burnout and resentment.

As we work on your impostor syndrome, you will have to constantly keep in mind that aspects of impostor syndrome, like overworking and perfectionism, are not badges of honor. Instead, they are blocks to fully appreciating all your skills and abilities. They are a mask covering your talents, skills, and experiences rather than the reason you have succeeded. Do not allow yourself, your self-esteem, or your personal life to be at their mercy.

WAYS TO RELEASE PERFECTIONISM

- Focus on "good enough" not perfect.
- Recognize that perfectionism hurts you and those around you.
- Be proud and accepting of your humanity.
- Only compare yourself to you.
- Find comfort in choosing your own path.
- Learn to accept the beauty of compromise.
- Choose standards that feel reasonable.
- Appreciate mistakes provide opportunity for growth.
- Realize that perfection is unattainable and reaching for it makes you feel like a failure.

GENDER DIFFERENCES

While the research does not show that impostor syndrome is significantly more prominent in men or women, it does suggest that there may be gender differences in the way that it manifests. As discussed earlier, men demonstrate a tendency toward underperforming, avoiding goals and feedback, and using peers who are less skilled as a comparison group when they are struggling with impostor syndrome. This then affects them by decreasing the likelihood for promotions and advancement over their lifetime, and reducing salary.[8] Men may feel a

8   Kumar and Jagacinski, "Impostors Have Goals Too," 147–57; Neureiter and Traut-Mattausch, "An Inner Barrier to Career Development," 37–48.

pull to save face and to conform to gender norms by doing work that they know how to do and will be successful at, rather than take the chance of failing and suffering the resulting self-esteem blow. Coping with the impostor syndrome by underperforming also reduces the feelings of anxiety, fear, and discomfort that impostor syndrome induces because there are fewer chances of feeling like an impostor.

For women, it's quite the opposite. Women seem to take the leap into the challenge, which often heightens the impostor syndrome. Women who struggle with impostor syndrome spend more time on academic tasks than those without impostor syndrome,[9] work harder when they receive negative feedback,[10] and have higher GPAs than men with impostor syndrome.[11] A 2018 study by Lauren A. Blondeau and Germine H. Awad,[12] found that having low self-efficacy and impostor syndrome did not impede a woman from pursuing a STEM career. Her GPA and interests were more influential to her choice. When men had high impostor syndrome scores in the study, they were less likely to pursue a STEM career. This shows a definite tendency for women to be counterphobic (i.e., facing fears directly) when it comes to impostor syndrome fears, which leaves them steeped in the constant experiences of feeling like an impostor.

In both ways of coping, the significant impact of impostor syndrome on your future and current functioning is pretty clear. Either you get the relief immediately by underperforming and avoiding or you are counterphobic and experience all the intense impostor feelings as you continue to accomplish, but don't get the relief because you discount these successes, which leaves you constantly under the weight of the impostor syndrome. Hopefully, this makes it really clear why building your skills around dismantling the impostor syndrome is incredibly important to you and your future so that you can own your greatness, live up to your potential, and enjoy it.

WHAT IS YOUR TYPICAL IMPOSTOR RESPONSE?

In this space indicate whether you tend to avoid or engage the tasks that you fear due to your experience of impostor syndrome. Then consider if/when you notice the alternative response. For example, I tend to engage the tasks that prompt impostor syndrome, but if there is potential for conflict in the task, then I will tend to avoid it.

---

9   King and Cooley, "Achievement Orientation and the Impostor Phenomenon," 304–12.

10   Badawy et al., "Are All Impostors Created Equal?" 155–63.

11   Cokley et al., "The Roles of Gender Stigma," 414–26.

12   Blondeau and Awad, "The Relation of the Impostor Phenomenon to Future Intentions," 253–67.

_____

_____

_____

THE IMPACT OF CULTURE

Impostor syndrome becomes harder to cope with when the stereotypes about your cultural group reinforce the notion that you are not "good enough." In marginalized communities, when your mere presence evokes concern that you have been given special treatment to be present in certain environments, the environment is telling you that you are an impostor. This makes overcoming your impostor syndrome particularly difficult because your accomplishments are actively disqualified (e.g., "you only attended that school because of affirmative action" or "they needed to diversify the team"). These are things you not only hear, but also experience when an organization further supports the idea that you are an impostor by over- or underutilizing you (e.g., not staffing you on important and internally visible teams or projects despite demanding your presence for public-facing pictures or for diversity initiatives). These types of microaggressions and microinsults at work can lead to entrenching the impostor syndrome because the external proof that you need to show yourself that you are not an impostor is harder to find.

Similarly, the concept of "stereotype threat" is useful to understand here as well. Stereotype threat is conforming to a well-known stereotype of a group you belong to when someone invokes the stereotype. In a very famous seminal study of stereotype threat conducted in 1995 by Claude Steele[13] from Stanford University and Joshua Aronson of University of Texas at Austin, these researchers found that Black college students scored significantly worse on standardized testing when they were told by an examiner that Black students would complete fewer questions and that it was an assessment of personal qualities. When the Black students were simply given instructions for the standardized tests, they scored similarly to the White students in the study. What Steele and Aronson, as well as hundreds of other researchers, were able to establish is that evoking a stereotype, sometimes even without words, can create diminished performance. Stereotype threat has been thought to contribute to gender and racial academic achievement gaps.

---

13   Steele and Aronson, "Stereotype Threat."

Now, imagine someone with impostor syndrome and from a marginalized group experiencing this stereotyping. This further impacts her performance as well as her anticipation of performing, perhaps further cementing the thoughts and insecurities that underlie impostor syndrome. Research has suggested that overcoming impostor syndrome for marginalized groups requires, besides the steps that we will cover in this book, a connection to and the ability to embrace the marginalized identity and the people who are similarly identified. It means not only connecting with those similar to you in this identity group, but also believing the counter narrative to the stereotype.

For example, if you are Black, the stereotypes that you are not academically capable have a long history of being ingrained in a cultural understanding of who deserves to be in the room and of meritocracy. Those beliefs are so perpetuated that often they are internalized by Black people, leading to beliefs that question other Black people's worthiness, academic ability, and intellectual rigor. To overcome impostor syndrome, you have to work to connect with other Black people and the belief that their worthiness is not in question. When you question the competence of other people with similar salient identities, you challenge your own (even if only on an unconscious level). When you can believe in their competence and give them the benefit of the doubt, you can believe in your own.

Besides race and gender, various other identities (e.g., religion, immigration status, sexual orientation, economic, and veteran status), as well as the intersectionality and salience of particular identities, should be considered as you examine how identity has impacted your development of impostor syndrome. For example, if you are a recent immigrant, you may want to understand the relevance of your immigration journey on the experience of feeling fraudulent in certain circumstances, especially if you have felt that this identity impacts your ability to internalize your accomplishments.

In this chapter, we have outlined the characteristics that underlie impostor syndrome and examined how it may manifest differently based on gender. We have also laid out the additional cultural aspects of overcoming impostor syndrome and how it can apply to a marginalized group, where competence is questioned as a result of stereotypes. Now, it's time to examine the important aspects of impostor syndrome that are most relevant for you.

THE KEY FEATURES OF YOUR IMPOSTOR SYNDROME

Review signs of impostor syndrome on page 4 as well as any other salient components of impostor syndrome that you have. This can include any potential gender, racial, ethnic, or other identity considerations. List them on the next page:

_____

_____

_____

_____

_____

_____

_____

YOUR IMPOSTOR SYNDROME INTENSITY

After you have completed your own assessment of the features of impostor syndrome that are specific to your experience, take Clance's test for impostor phenomenon, which you can find here: http://paulineroseclance.com/impostor_phenomenon.html.

Once you have scored your assessment, circle your current level of impostor feelings:

FEW   MODERATE   FREQUENT   INTENSE

Reviewing your current level of impostor feelings is helpful in understanding the present impact of impostor syndrome on your life and career. If you score in the few to moderate range, this may be a great time to tackle the book because you are not feeling impostor syndrome in its most pressing state. This will allow you to look back at experiences when your impostor feelings were more powerful, and analyze and review them from a distance. If you are experiencing impostor syndrome at the frequent to intense range, this likely suggests that impostor syndrome is quite salient for you right now. You may have plenty of experiences that are coming up for you that you will be able to pull from and directly impact as you work through this book.

THE 3 C's STRATEGY TO OVERCOMING IMPOSTOR SYNDROME

Overcoming impostor syndrome can be a challenging proposition, especially when faced with a stressful work or personal environment. It may feel impossible to eliminate these thoughts and feelings of being a fraud, and you may always be on edge about being exposed.

Jocelyn was someone who constantly had such feelings. She was a management consultant who had worked in her field for several years and was on the partner track. Jocelyn worked long hours and traveled extensively. She had no social life and rarely saw her family, with whom she was very close. She came to seek coaching because she was thinking about making a career change. Despite receiving glowing performance reviews every year, Jocelyn felt like an impostor and was always concerned that she would be fired or be asked to leave her firm. Her manager would often tell her how well she was doing, but it did not convince her. She dreaded Mondays because she anticipated the miserable commute, the constant anxiety during her work hours, and the grind of the day. During the course of coaching, we identified that a good deal of her work stress was due to her impostor syndrome. Until we named it as such, Jocelyn thought these feelings of self-doubt were just part of her personality and could not be changed. She was relieved to find out that it was something that could be addressed and changed.

Fortunately, we developed the 3 C's (Clarify, Choose, and Create) Strategy, which helped Jocelyn and can also help you alleviate fears and self-doubt, and vanquish your impostor syndrome. This chapter will provide a brief overview of the 3 C's Strategy, and subsequent chapters will explore each phase of the strategy in more depth, with corresponding activities to help you master its application to live your best life possible.

We have used the 3 C's Strategy as a framework during our more than 15 years in practice to help our clients overcome impostor syndrome. While impostor syndrome is not a diagnosable disorder, we have found that by using the 3 C's strategy, our clients are able to diminish their impostor syndrome thoughts, feelings, and behaviors to improve the quality of their work and personal lives.

The 3 C's Strategy involves reflecting on all aspects of your life, some of which you may not have considered (e.g., your self-constructed narrative), as well as clearly identifying factors that may have influenced the development of your impostor syndrome (e.g., family dynamics). It also prompts you to actively engage with others about your impostor syndrome rather than suffering with it in silent shame. While you may periodically have those impostor syndrome thoughts and feelings, applying the 3 C's Strategy will cause them to occur less frequently and have less of an influence on your behavior.

Each of the three phases of the 3 C's Strategy contains three steps, for a total of nine steps. When working with our clients, we tend to move through the phases in a sequential manner, with tangible activities to complete in each area. There is no set time period to move through the phases, but it is important to remain consistently focused on the tasks required for each phase. Such consistency will facilitate your ability to apply the strategy for its maximum effectiveness.

The 3 C's Model

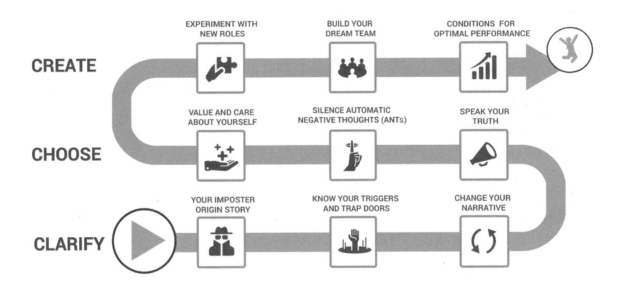

The 3 C's strategy will be a key tool to help you overcome impostor syndrome. By progressing through each step within each phase, you will build confidence, change your thinking, create a more positive narrative, and finally own your greatness. When your impostor syndrome rears its ugly head, you will be well-equipped to spot it, neutralize it, and continue on your road to living in the glory of your accomplishments and excitement about your future.

Chapters 2 through 4 will review Phase 1 (Clarify) and the first three steps of the 3C's strategy, which are knowing your origin story, identifying your triggers, and changing your narrative. Chapters 5 through 7 will examine Phase 2 (Choose) and the next three steps, which are speak your truth, silence automatic negative thoughts, and value your self-care. Chapters 8 through 10 will cover Phase 3 (Create), and the final three steps of the 3C's strategy, which include experimenting with new roles, establishing your dream team, and understanding the optimal conditions for your success.

In these next chapters, we are going to outline our program for overcoming your impostor syndrome. We will lay out the 3 C's Strategy to put an end to the way that impostor syndrome impacts your life, your view of your accomplishments, and your performance and advancement. We are going to help you to feel a sense of control and a reduction in fear of being revealed as a fraud. Once you can really own your greatness, you are going to be unstoppable!

KEY TAKEAWAYS

- You understand the key components of impostor syndrome.

- You comprehend its impact on career and work.

- You have learned how gender may impact impostor syndrome.

- You see how stereotyping around culture and identity can impact the perpetual impostor syndrome.

- You have evaluated your own level of impostor syndrome.

- You understand the brief overview of the 3C's Strategy.

PHASE ONE
CLARIFY

Chapter 2

STEP 1: IDENTIFY YOUR IMPOSTOR SYNDROME ORIGIN STORY

Clarify represents an opportunity to tell yourself a different story. People with impostor syndrome often repeat negative stories to themselves, which usually portray them as a fraud and incompetent. The first part of developing a new story is to understand your impostor syndrome origin story. When did you first become aware of these impostor feelings? Was it in high school? College? Or was it when you first entered the professional workforce or earned your first promotion? It may have even been earlier when you were a young child. Identifying your impostor syndrome origin story means exploring possible connections between your family dynamics, including the messages communicated to you about your abilities, and the development of your impostor syndrome. It also can involve examining how cultural context, including discrimination based on expectations of underperformance and/or stereotypes, may have also shaped your impostor syndrome. By gaining this insight, you can begin to truly understand the possible root causes of impostor syndrome and start on the path to vanquishing it.

As psychologists, we believe that knowing your history and really understanding the origins of a negative pattern can help you to pinpoint your triggers and finally and decisively end that pattern. In this chapter, we are going to help you dig into your own history and your family's story so that you can observe and be aware of how your impostor syndrome came to be. With this knowledge, you will recognize that changing is an amazing task that you are undertaking to dismantle years, sometimes generations, of the feeling of fraudulence. Not only can eradicating the pattern in yourself be monumentally important, but once you have the skills and methods to rid yourself of the impostor syndrome, you also have the power to prevent it in the next generation as you will be conscious of the behaviors, messages, and dynamics that create it. You can avoid parenting, mentoring, and supervising in ways that elicit impostor syndrome, you can support others in their process of eliminating impostor syndrome, and you can model healthy habits and behaviors to show what owning your greatness can look like. You can break a family cycle of impostor syndrome by just changing yours.

Before we start, we want to teach you some of the important familial and development hallmarks of the creation of impostor syndrome so that you can clearly identify them when you see them in your own history. Then we will ask you to identify them exactly as they occurred in your own experience. These are likely the foundation of your triggers. Once identified, it becomes easier to notice the trigger when it occurs in the here and now.

FAMILY DYNAMICS

Clance and Imes identified some of the following family dynamics that were hallmark of those that they followed with impostor syndrome.[14] They had either:

- A sibling or close family member deemed as the "intelligent" member of the family. On the other hand, the person with impostor syndrome was considered the sensitive or social/emotionally competent family member.

  Sometimes, being social and emotionally aware and competent aren't really hailed as positive characteristics, and being labeled as such can be seen as being overly emotional or valuing emotions more than one should. No matter what this child does, he/she can never prove as intelligent as the identified sibling or family member even if their objective performance at school is better. She is hoping that she will get acknowledged for her intelligence over emotional awareness, but this acknowledgment rarely, if ever, comes. She is given this role in the family and cannot break out of it or expand it. She doubts whether she is intelligent and attributes the success to her social skills and her ability to understand the teacher's criteria for excelling in the class.

---

14   Cokley et al., 2013 "An Examination of the Impact of Minority Status," 82–95; Bernard et al., "Racial Discrimination, Racial Identity, and Impostor Phenomenon."

- The family conveys the message that the child is superior in every way—intellect, social skills, and so on. The ease with which she does things is admired.

  In this scenario, her precociousness as a child is noted and valued, and there are resulting high expectations. The way she perceives this is that everything should come easy. As a result, the first time she has to work at anything, it shatters her understanding of her intellect. It feels fraudulent if she has to study hard or try hard at anything. If she is not a genius, then she is an impostor.

Throughout our years of working with clients, we have noticed a third family dynamic, which is also prevalent:

- The child is gifted intellectually or driven to succeed from an early age with parents who are neglectful, abusive, or absent.

  In this experience, the child is driven to succeed due to his family circumstances and has rarely received positive feedback from parental figures, so he finds it difficult to take in compliments and overworks constantly due to his concern that if he stops, everything will fall apart.

Besides these dynamics, here are some other factors that have been connected with the development of impostor syndrome:

- Achievement, especially in academic or professional settings, is highly valued in the family and is the main or primary source of validation

- Anger and conflict are present and not well managed in the family

- Communication and behavior in the home are governed by strict rules and procedures on how things are done

- Support for the individual child and his/her individual, unique, complex experiences and skills is lacking

- High need to please others in the family

- High need to control impulses (for women)

- Low need to control impulses (for men)

While the last two dynamics have been seen predominantly in certain genders, it is possible for you to exhibit the one that has not been seen in your gender. For example, you might be a man with impostor syndrome that has extreme control of your impulses.

Finally, when you are thinking about your family dynamics, sometimes they are organized in either a narcissistic or codependent way.

Narcissistic family dynamics tend to be organized around the needs of a particular family member, sometimes more than one. The children are required to fulfill their parent(s)' needs and wishes, and this is often controlled by validation only around domains that the parent(s) finds worthy. The child is molded to meet the parent(s)' expectations. When the child fails to meet these expectations, there are significant consequences, which feel like the loss of the parent(s)' love or attention. You can see this experience is very similar to the impostor syndrome dynamic of feeling like a fraud if you are caught in a mistake or exposed as lacking in some way.

Codependent families are usually organized around the illness (diagnosed or undiagnosed) of a particular identified problem person(s) that creates intense emergencies or fragility. Some of the key dynamics can support the development of impostor syndrome. First, the child may have needed to overregulate his/her own emotions because the "identified problem person" in the family takes up significant space. In addition, the family promotes dependence over autonomy, as well as the denial of one's needs. For example, you may be recruited to support the care of an adult sibling, even though this sibling may be fully capable of caring for themselves. The types of symptoms that are often seen in members of families with high levels of codependence include fear, anxiety, low self-esteem, and depression, which mimic a lot of the symptoms seen in people with impostor syndrome. Looking for approval from others, having trouble expressing your own opinions, and feeling insecure of your own accomplishments are natural developments from these conditions. In the example of Ashten, you see some of these family dynamics at play in how her impostor syndrome exhibits itself:

> *Ashten is a 35-year-old senior leader at a nonprofit, but she has struggled with her worthiness to hold influential roles at organizations. Currently, this is further exacerbated by having a critical supervisor who never praises her, is constantly picking at small issues, and expects Ashten to be at her beck and call at all hours of the day and night. As Ashten thinks about her family history, she shares: "I was always considered 'the great hope' for my family. My oldest brother has always been in trouble. He likely has some undiagnosed mental health issue. My sister also*

never went to college and always has some relationship crisis going on. My mother is constantly trying to get me to help them and is overly involved in the difficulties in their lives, even though they're in their forties, and it's exhausting. My achievements have always been the focus of my worth to my family. I went to a magnet school and my school experiences never included anything fun. My parents were constantly asking about every grade and test and nothing under an A was acceptable. Then, I went to an Ivy League university for college. I have always felt my professional life was fragile and that any moment, I was going to be found out. Then, it all would disappear and I would be back home living in the chaos of my family. My parents are always trying to manipulate me to come home and help out, either with money or emotional support for my siblings. But I don't want to go home, due to the chaos with my siblings and my parents constantly arguing. There are many codependent relationships in my family, with my brother and sister largely being the focus. There may also be some narcissistic behavior going on, especially around expectations, which I am just now beginning to notice. I am afraid that underneath all the education and accomplishments, I am just like them—and if I don't overwork at every moment, it will all fall apart."

Now, we want you to think about the family dynamics that were relevant for you as a child and perhaps continue as an adult.

IDENTIFY YOUR FAMILY DYNAMICS

Listed below and on the next page are some of the common family dynamics involved in the development of impostor syndrome. Take the time now to identify and check all the ones that resonate for you. This exercise is the first step in identifying triggers for your impostor syndrome in the present day.

❏ You are considered the social/emotionally competent one.

❏ You were told that you had natural gifts and talent that didn't require effort.

❏ Academic or professional achievement is highly valued in your family.

❏ Anger and conflict are present and not well managed in the family.

❏ Communication and behavior are governed by strict rules and procedures.

❑ Your individual, unique, and complex experiences are not supported.

❑ High need to please others in the family.

❑ High need to control impulses OR low need to control impulses.

❑ Narcissistic family dynamics.

❑ Codependent family dynamics.

It is also useful to review where these dynamics existed and their generational nature. In the next activity, we are going to ask you to draw the representation of these dynamics in your family system using a family genogram method.

LEGEND OF GENOGRAM SYMBOLS

Here are some simple genogram symbols from *Genograms: Assessment and Intervention*, so you can develop a genogram of your relevant family dynamics.

Basic Genogram Symbols

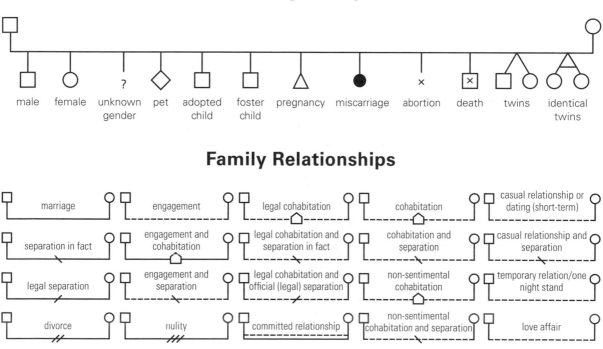

Family Relationships

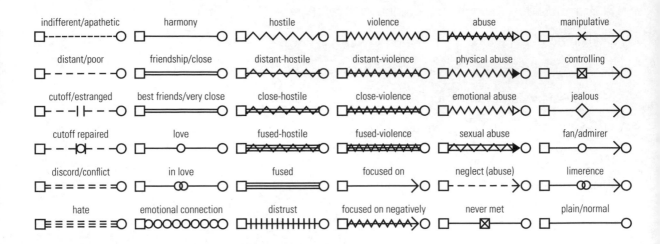

indifferent/apathetic	harmony	hostile	violence	abuse	manipulative
distant/poor	friendship/close	distant-hostile	distant-violence	physical abuse	controlling
cutoff/estranged	best friends/very close	close-hostile	close-violence	emotional abuse	jealous
cutoff repaired	love	fused-hostile	fused-violence	sexual abuse	fan/admirer
discord/conflict	in love	fused	focused on	neglect (abuse)	limerence
hate	emotional connection	distrust	focused on negatively	never met	plain/normal

ASHTEN'S SAMPLE GENOGRAM

Here's the sample genogram of Ashten, the 35-year-old woman with impostor syndrome that we discussed on page 23. We have highlighted the pieces of her family description that connect to the aspects of family dynamics seen with people who have impostor syndrome. She illustrates her genogram below:

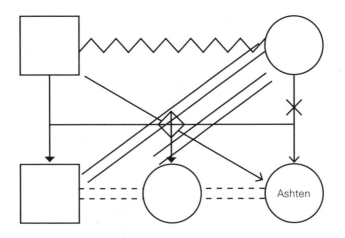

You see in her diagram that her mother is particularly close or fused with her older brother and sister. There is conflict among the siblings and the parents. You can also visualize the impact of her feelings that her father is controlling of her and her mother is manipulative of her. These types of visual representations can be useful in understanding patterns in your family.

YOUR IMPOSTOR SYNDROME FAMILY DYNAMICS

It's your turn to draw your family genogram and then describe it with a focus on the family dynamics that affected the development of your impostor syndrome. Then, go back over your drawing and describe the particular pieces of the family dynamics that relate to your impostor syndrome (similar to the example above).

- You understand the link between your impostor syndrome and your family dynamics.

- You identified your particular family dynamics that fostered the impostor syndrome.

- You began to narrate your story.

- You increased your awareness of your possible triggers for impostor syndrome.

Chapter 3

STEP 2: KNOW YOUR IMPOSTOR SYNDROME TRIGGERS

The next part of the Clarify phase is to identify your impostor syndrome triggers, situations which increase or activate your impostor feelings and thoughts. One of the most typical triggers is being placed in a new situation. For instance, if you are promoted to a new leadership position, you may begin to have more active impostor syndrome feelings, such as doubt about your ability to handle the new role. You may think that you don't deserve this opportunity, will soon be discovered as incompetent, and will be quickly fired. Compliments can be another trigger. Rather than fully appreciating and internalizing the affirmation, your impostor syndrome thoughts lead you to believe that the person is "just being nice," but must surely know that your work is subpar and that you are not very capable. These triggers may prevent you from exploring new opportunities, such as starting a business, changing jobs, or asking for a promotion.

Although a good deal of impostor syndrome experiences and triggers occur in the workplace, they can also appear in your personal life, especially when you start a new relationship or enter new social situations. You may doubt how much your new partner or friend values you or cares about you. This can inhibit how you engage with them, inevitably causing tension in your relationships. For instance, you might be skeptical of your partner's compliments and unable to accept them graciously. Or you may believe that your friend or your partner doesn't really know who you are, and when they do, they will end your relationship. Or you might stay in unhealthy social relationships because you feel that you may not be likable enough to find more suitable companions.

By identifying triggers, you can be more aware of how impostor syndrome might influence you and begin to respond proactively to neutralize it.

This chapter will help you to identify and solidly understand your triggers so that you can begin to intervene and challenge the ways in which these triggers have been framed. You can then develop some new narratives about these triggers.

You are not likely experiencing impostor syndrome at every moment that you are faced with something difficult. There are probably aspects of your life that you feel quite competent doing. It may be that you feel like you are a great friend, or skilled at organizing. It's important to recognize when you are good at certain things, especially in conditions where the triggers don't exist. The example below of Sung, a 42-year-old talent manager, demonstrates how important it is to be aware of your competencies:

> *Sung is incredibly skilled at assessing talent and knowing where a person will excel in the organization. She is responsible for assigning consultants to projects. Recently, she's gotten some opportunities as a result of her skill in this area. While she experiences impostor syndrome in other aspects of her life, her competencies in this area are not well appreciated, although they are not the source of her impostor feelings.*

YOUR COMPETENCIES TODAY

Create a list of three to five things that you feel competent in or where you perform well. How have these skills been positive for you? Are these experiences impostor-free? If so, why do you think this is?

1. _____

_____

_____

_____

2. _____

_____

_____

_____

3. _____

_____

_____

_____

4. _____

_____

_____

_____

5. _____

_____

_____

_____

• • •

The image on page 32 is a wonderfully simple explanation of how a stressful trigger can affect us. At the top, you are exposed to a stressor. This is filtered through your perception, which, for those with impostor syndrome, is influenced by your family dynamics and your narrative. Then, you decide if the stressor is positive, dangerous, or irrelevant. The stressors relevant to your impostor syndrome are likely to be seen as dangerous. From here, you decide if you have enough resources to deal with it. You will then go through the coping strategies—either problem-focused, emotion-focused, or wise mind, which is a combination of both. Without the proper tools, people tend to be reactive or solve the wrong problem. At the end of this process, you will take another look at the situation in reappraisal and assess what you did well and what you could do better the next time that you face the stressor or trigger. With impostor syndrome, the cycle continues to repeat because there is no reappraisal at the end of the cycle. Hopefully, after reading this book, you will no longer do this, and you will be constantly learning how to improve the way you handle your impostor syndrome triggers.

Lazarus's Transactional Model of Stress

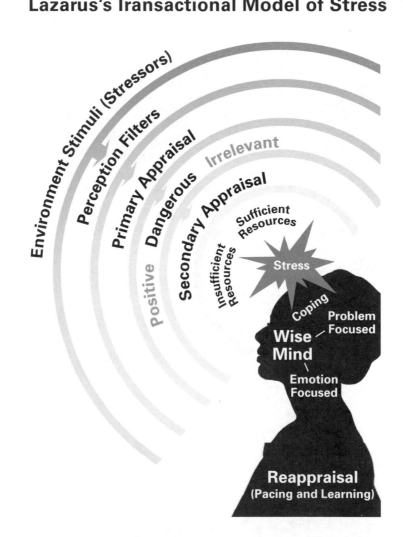

Typically, particular situations, people, and places trigger you and allow you to fall into the trapdoor of impostor syndrome. Understanding exactly what these triggers are will help you to identify them in the moment and choose a different reaction rather than fall into impostor syndrome. Let's begin to examine what those triggers may be.

IMPOSTOR SCENARIOS

Describe a few recent impactful situations where your impostor syndrome was particularly difficult for you. When have you recently felt like a fraud? Were you concerned about being exposed? Did you feel intense fears about losing a role, status, or the opportunity for a special experience? Have you found yourself overworking or avoiding in some circumstance?

_____

_____

_____

_____

_____

_____

_____

_____

_____

_____

_____

_____

Now, after writing out these scenarios, do you notice any themes? What do they have in common? Is there an emotional state, behavior, thought, place, thing, scenario, or person that incited the impostor syndrome? It might be more than one trigger. Use the chart on the next page to brainstorm and then identify by circling or highlighting the commonalities.

SCENARIO	TRIGGER	COMMON THEMES

EMOTIONAL STATE	
BEHAVIOR	
THOUGHT	
PLACE	
THING	
SCENARIO	
PERSON	

OWN YOUR GREATNESS

Now, I want you to integrate what you have learned about the trigger into a statement. Let's put what you have learned into narrative form.

When my impostor syndrome is activated, I am usually:

feeling _____

_____

thinking _____

_____

behaving in ways _____

_____

and I am triggered by:

situations that _____

_____

places that _____

_____

people who _____

_____

things that _____

_____

Through these exercises, you want to begin to have a clear picture of what your particular triggers are and what state you are in when you are triggered and engage your impostor syndrome to cope.

WHY YOUR TRIGGERS EXIST

Now that you have a clearer picture, let's work backward and look at *why* these are your triggers so you can begin to dismantle some of their power. It's not random chance that these are your triggers. They likely are a result of some earlier instances in your life when you felt incompetent and not good enough.

So, let's look back to your origin story from the previous chapter as well as reflect on early experiences where you see similarities. For example, you might have noted through the exercises that you tend to be triggered toward engaging in an impostor way when a supervisor has a leadership style that offers very little positive feedback. Through doubting your skill and your ability to perform, you feel like you are in an unending cycle of constantly having to prove yourself. When you reflect back, you may realize that your father tended to withhold positive feedback and often questioned whether you were capable of challenging academic experiences. We want you to identify where these patterns originate and where the initial feeling of fraudulence or incompetence came from.

TRIGGER ORIGINS

In this activity, catalog all the experiences that you have discovered as you reflect on your origin story.

The triggers that I experience today started when:

- _____

_____

_____

_____

_____

- _____

_____

_____

_____

- _____

_____

_____

_____

_____

● ● ●

Now we know what triggers you in the here and now and we have a sense of where these triggers came from. Next, we want to lighten their emotional impact so that they don't override your ability to be nonreactive in your coping (or at least less reactive) when they are triggered in your everyday life.

THE EXPRESSIVE LETTER

In this activity, you are going to write a letter to the person that you see as mainly driving the events related to your triggers. If it is more than one person, each person gets their own letter. Write to this person about what you feel regarding their role in the dynamics that spurred on your impostor syndrome. Express every feeling, instance that you remember, and perhaps even the ways it still continues.

The following important components to your letter(s) will make this exercise effective in helping you move on:

- It must be handwritten—the process of handwriting engages more parts of your brain and your emotional experience.

- You will have some space on the next page to start the letter, but you will likely have more to say so please continue writing this letter on separate sheets of paper until you feel like you have said everything you need to say or you find yourself repeating yourself.

- Feel free to say anything you need to say in this letter. Do not censor yourself in any way. Use whatever language you need to. Don't worry about punctuation, tense, capitalization, and so on.

- Write in stream of consciousness—whatever comes out, that's what you write. There is no need to organize the material in chronological order.

- Once you complete the bulk of the letter sharing your feelings about their role in these dynamics, write a statement about forgiving them. You should not write this statement until you are truly ready to forgive this person and let go.

- Sign the letter.

Once you have completed the letter, read it out loud to someone you trust, who can truly witness and take in what you share in the letter and keep it confidential. When you have read the letter out loud to your trusted person, destroy the letter in some way that feels cathartic, as if you can feel in the destruction that you are letting go of everything in that letter.

For some of our clients, it takes both sides of seven to eight pages of legal-size paper to complete these letters. Often, clients forget to write the forgiveness statement. You must complete the forgiveness statement before reading it aloud to your confidant. It can be a very emotional process that can take stops and starts to complete. You do not have to finish it in one sitting. But if you take the exercise seriously, it can be a very powerful tool to let go and move forward, and that's what you need before you take on the next steps.

_____

_____

_____

_____

_____

_____

_____

_____

_____

FACING TRIGGERS IN THE HERE AND NOW

By now, we hope you know your triggers inside and out. There should be no secret or hidden triggers at this point because to know your trigger is to have the power to react to them differently than you have in past. In the past, these triggers made you feel like a fraud, less than, and incompetent, but now, you will know them simply as an old trigger.

Now that you have identified your triggers, their origins, and addressed them to let them go, what happens when you experience a familiar trigger in your everyday experience? In the next few chapters, we are going to give you all kinds of tools that you can employ, instead of responding in impostor-inducing ways like catering to the needs of others, and denying your own experiences and accomplishments, and coping with the fear of being found out by overworking or avoiding.

KEY TAKEAWAYS

- You're aware of your competencies, skills, and accomplishments.

- You can identify your major triggers and the components of these triggers, including characteristics of the people, places, situations, and emotional states that trigger your impostor syndrome.

- You identified a person or people that were integral to the development of your impostor syndrome and worked to tell your story and to let go and forgive those involved.

- You understand that knowing your triggers allows you to respond differently to the trigger instead of with impostor syndrome coping skills (e.g., overworking or avoiding).

Chapter 4

STEP 3: CHANGE YOUR NARRATIVE

The final part of Clarify is changing your narrative, the story that you tell yourself, which keeps you filled with self-doubt and a negative perception of yourself. Your narrative has a great deal of power in keeping impostor syndrome central to your identity, or freeing you from it.

Jocelyn's narrative (from page 16) was that she was lucky to have her job, and that the primary reasons she was able to keep it was due to her hard work and her pleasant demeanor. Her narrative neglects the fact that she finished in the top 5 percent of her class in college, excelled in her role as an intern at the firm, and consistently received praise about both her technical and soft skills. This distorted narrative served to preserve Jocelyn's impostor syndrome beliefs and caused her to avoid seeking a better-fitting and more-satisfying job.

You may also have such distorted narratives about the reasons for your success. You may believe that you were just lucky. Or that no one else really wanted the role. Or that a mistake was made, and that a better candidate was overlooked. Such narratives enable the impostor syndrome beliefs to stay intact, and you continue to feel less than worthy of your achievements.

Although it may be difficult to do initially, changing your narrative involves acknowledging your achievements, identifying the distortions in your story, and claiming a more positive, complex, thickened, and balanced story.

This chapter will discuss how to craft a more realistic and affirming narrative, and how to internalize it in order to overcome impostor syndrome and live a more satisfying life. We will explore the key factors to changing your narrative, including highlighting your positive attributes, strengths, skills, and accomplishments.

The stories that we tell ourselves about a situation have a great impact on what we choose to do next in situations that dictate the trajectory of our lives. The date, particular people present, and the location of the situation are all examples of objective facts. However, how you interpret the situation can vary widely from how someone else might and is affected by a whole variety of factors. What's important to know is that while you can't change your past, you can change your understanding of it, which is so much more important and powerful to how you take on your future. To rethink the way that you narrate your life and the way that you interpret the experiences around you gives you incredible leverage to change the nature of your perspective and how you can free yourself from the grips of impostor syndrome.

Narrative therapy is an approach to change that was developed in the 1980s by Michael White and David Epston, two therapists from New Zealand. It is focused on separating the individuals from the problem, and allowing them to externalize their issue, in order to take a greater sense of control around the stories in their life. In this way, they are no longer the victim in the narrative, but rather the hero. Techniques from this approach are so valuable for people struggling with impostor syndrome because of a pervasive tendency in them to internalize all negative issues as relating to a deficiency in themselves or something they did wrong. When you are contending with impostor syndrome, you can struggle to internalize all the positives that occur or are attributed to you.

One of the first steps of the narrative technique is to simply tell your story, which you did in Chapter 2. Your next step will be to identify the characteristics that are particularly triggering for you using an exercise we have adapted from narrative therapy called "Statement of Position Map."

STATEMENT OF POSITION MAP

Step 1: Reflect on Your Story

Looking back at your responses from Chapter 3: Identify Your Impostor Syndrome Origin Story, what are the key components of your story that feed your impostor syndrome? Try to list as many as you can. What are the key family dynamics that you were exposed to (e.g., were you considered the smart one?)? What other issues were at play for you? Did you have a high need to please others? Was your family very achievement oriented? Did your family have narcissistic or codependent features?

- _____
- _____
- _____
- _____
- _____

Step 2: Map the Effects of Impostor Syndrome on Each Domain of Your Life

How do the components identified in Step 1 currently affect the following domains of your life? For example, if achievement was highly valued in your family, do you notice yourself preoccupied with looking for the next promotion at work to feel valued? If there were narcissistic features in your household, do you notice that you tend to have narcissistic bosses that you can never please? Think about how the origin issues relate to what's currently happening in your life around your impostor syndrome.

HOME:

_____

_____

_____

WORK:

_____

_____

_____

SCHOOL:

_____

_____

_____

RELATIONSHIPS:

_____

_____

_____

STEP 3: Reflect on Why Effects Are Undesirable

Take some time now to think about why these effects are working against you. What do you really want? How are your values being compromised by the effects of impostor syndrome on your life?

_____

_____

_____

_____

_____

• • •

One of the techniques that comes from a narrative therapy approach that is very powerful in altering your perspective is *thickening a narrative*. The idea is to take a thin and simplistic point of view about a story that you have come to accept, and narrate it in a way that gives it more thickness, complexity, and perhaps more accuracy in relation to your experience and the way it plays out in your life today. Thin descriptions are often created and provided by others, usually those who have power to define particular circumstances, like parents, teachers, and other authority figures. These thin descriptions, however, lack in context and can be powerful motivators for behavior and can sustain and support often negative and destructive actions in our lives.

For example, if your family story around your intelligence was, "I am the one who works hard, but my sister, Sam, is the smart one." This type of narrative could lead to thinking that the only value you are allowed to show is to work hard, which leads to a workaholic lifestyle, lack of balance, little attention to your personal life, and distinct periods of burnout. To thicken this narrative, you might add other components, "Both Sam and I are intelligent. The way we go about learning and expressing our understanding is different. I like to write and study what I have written and Sam learns and retains oral communication. So, it looks like she doesn't have to try, but this is the way she is learning." Now, this challenges the perspective that only Sam is smart. You can both be intelligent and have had different skills. One may look like it is "natural and requires no effort" and the other like it takes a lot of work, so you aren't as intellectually gifted. Thickening this narrative allows you to use the skills that boost your learning, like using a notepad in meetings and requiring some time to respond back to an issue that was raised, rather than have the perfect statement ready in the moment, without feeling ashamed.

Thickening a story can give you new alternatives and outcomes. It can take the shame out of things that are totally normal. It can help you to see context and add richness to your understanding of your process. Thickening a narrative requires looking at the original story that you tell yourself and really questions its premises. It can require you to challenge ideas that while simplistic, seem true, inevitable, and unquestionable. In order to thicken a narrative, you have to shift your perspective from objective reality (e.g., there is only one truth) to subjective reality (e.g., there are many truths, and each has its own merit and value.) You have to be able to recognize that there are multiple ways to tell a story and for you, the main purpose is to move more toward internalizing your positive characteristics that support ideas that you are intelligent, capable, and worthy of all that you have accomplished. You want to move away from stories that suggest that you need to constantly work hard, that you are only as good as your last performance, that you are a fraud and that your accomplishments are tenuous.

THICKENING YOUR STORY

Think about a statement that underlies your impostor syndrome, one that you tell yourself or that others have told about you and that you've incorporated into your understanding of yourself. Try to recall exactly how this is communicated, and then you thicken the narrative.

Original Story or Statement

_____

_____

_____

_____

_____

Take a second to review the original story or statement and think about its meaning. What does it allow you to believe about yourself? What are the particular outcomes that are possible from this story? How does it limit you?

_____

_____

_____

_____

_____

Thickened Story or Statement

How can you add to this story? Add more context? Make it richer and give it more dimension, even if that means there are contradictory elements in the story. For example, you can be strong and vulnerable simultaneously.

_____

_____

_____

_____

_____

What do you notice about your process of thickening your story? What did you have to do to thicken the story? When you say it out loud, how does that thickened statement feel? Do the two statements feel different? In what ways? How are the potential outcomes different if you think about yourself and your story in a thickened way?

_____

_____

_____

_____

_____

THE POWER OF BOTH-AND THINKING

In therapy, we talk about this concept constantly and it is important for the thickening exercise. The "both-and" allows you to consider two or more things to be possible when you have typically thought of them in an "either-or" manner.

You can feel happy for a friend, who has received a promotion, and also feel a sense of sadness because you are stuck at a job with no possibility for advancement.

You can hold both the happiness and sadness.

At this point in the book, you are hopefully beginning to see the power of your own voice in narrating your story and developing the outcomes that fit your values, your hopes, and your dreams for yourself. In the vein of narrating your story, now you are actually going to do that. In the next exercise, you are going to write your autobiography. In this activity, we want you to stretch the muscles that allow you to believe in the diverse possibilities for yourself. We want you to feel and think expansively and not narrowly about your life.

YOUR AUTOBIOGRAPHY

Come up with an autobiography title and at least seven chapter titles that capture your entire life. Use your new skills on thickening the narrative of your life to predict what will happen.

Autobiography Title:

_____

Chapter 1 Title:

_____

Description:_____

_____

_____

Chapter 2 Title:

_____

Description:_____

_____

_____

Chapter 3 Title:

_____

_____

Description:_____

_____

_____

Chapter 4 Title:

_____

Description: _____

_____

_____

Chapter 5 Title:

_____

Description: _____

_____

_____

Chapter 6 Title:

_____

Description: _____

_____

_____

Chapter 7 Title:

_____

Description: _____

_____

_____

After titling your autobiography and its chapters, write a short summary to describe the book to readers.

_____

_____

_____

_____

_____

● ● ●

It can be very difficult at first to narrate your story in a different way. You will have to think more consciously about what you tell others about your accomplishments and capacity. Speak more slowly, and catch and correct yourself when you say something to disparage or minimize your accomplishments, value your overwork, or perpetuate the notion that you are a fraud or not worthy. Take these skills into your everyday life and use them to give yourself new and varied possibilities for how your story proceeds. It will take work because these are new skills. Before they become automatic, they will require you to attend to your narrative with greater care and attention to the impact of your words and your story on your future.

KEY TAKEAWAYS

- You have an understanding of how impostor syndrome works in different aspects of your life.

- You have developed and are able to use "thickened" language when triggered around your impostor syndrome experience.

- You have created a new narrative and way to think about your life (past, present, and future) that is focused on your accomplishments, abilities, and possibilities.

PHASE TWO

CHOOSE

Chapter 5

STEP 4: SPEAK YOUR TRUTH

This phase, Choose, includes Steps 4 through 6. It is about making new choices in your life and taking steps forward from what you have learned in Phase 1, Clarify. You have just explored your origin story, learned your triggers, and worked on the creation of a new narrative. Now, in Phase 2, we will focus on the behaviors you will purposely employ to live in, breathe, and enjoy this new narrative.

Choose involves speaking your truth, silencing automatic negative thoughts, and valuing your own self-care. When you deal with impostor syndrome, it is often in silence, because you are embarrassed or ashamed. You may feel that you are the only one who experiences this, and therefore, no one will understand. Jocelyn struggled with the silence of impostor syndrome for years and thought that her family and friends, who viewed her as extremely successful, would think she was silly or ungrateful for her successes. Thus, she never spoke about her impostor feelings, which caused them to persist.

Speaking your truth means admitting and verbalizing your impostor syndrome anxieties and fears to trusted others. Doing so can immediately weaken it. It can also provide you with more support to battle it. Jocelyn was surprised to hear how many of her friends experienced similar feelings, when she began to disclose her impostor syndrome to them. Rather than ridiculing or admonishing her, they acknowledged the challenges and explored strategies to deal with impostor syndrome.

In addition to articulating your experience to others, speaking your truth means owning your achievements and strengths. Many individuals with impostor syndrome attribute any success to external sources, such as luck and people being nice to them. They often cannot identify accomplishments or strengths and tend to minimize or reject praise. Whether it is your recent promotion or being praised for your performance on an important project, owning your accomplishments will be a key element to overcoming impostor syndrome.

After some initial difficulty, Jocelyn was able to confidently identify key strengths, such as her communication skills, and several accomplishments, which bolstered her self-confidence and enabled her to weaken her impostor syndrome feelings.

One of the most difficult aspects of impostor syndrome is that people who suffer with it often do so in silence. In this phase of the 3 C's process of overcoming impostor syndrome, Choice will be the focus of your activities. Speaking your truth means you are making a conscious choice to confront and own the impostor syndrome head-on with help from trusted others.

There is no shame in admitting to experiencing impostor syndrome, as many high-achieving individuals struggle with it. In fact, it is estimated that 70 percent of people will experience one incident of impostor syndrome in their lives.[15] While it might be easier to offhandedly say to someone, "I've experienced impostor syndrome," it's usually much harder to share the actual experiences, triggers, emotions, and crippling thoughts that follow you. Talking about your impostor syndrome can be relieving and surprisingly bonding. You will likely find that other people in your life, whom you deeply respect, may identify with your distress. Speaking your truth means honoring your experience and accepting that defeating impostor syndrome is a process. That is the experience Lisa had when she wanted to quit a job, which was affecting her self-confidence and severely draining her:

> When Lisa was struggling to leave her role at a college, part of the challenge for her was that she felt ashamed and alone. She couldn't believe that she was in this embarrassing predicament. Lisa had worked so hard to earn her doctorate in psychology at Columbia University, and after so many years, she was in a low-level administrative role outside of her field, with few options for advancement. She was being humiliated in public by her boss. She was being paid far less than her counterpart, and there was no plan to remediate this. It was difficult for her to talk about her situation and, as a result, no one seemed to understand why she was stuck, which caused her to feel trapped and unable to move forward. Fortunately, Lisa was able to finally speak her truth, when her boss finally made a comment that

---

15 Gravois, "You're Not Fooling Anyone."

made her realize that she could not stay any longer. She found the courage to raise her outrage about her treatment to her family and friends, who encouraged her to quit. Voicing her impostor syndrome experience freed her to make the best decision for herself, to exit an unhealthy and unproductive situation and begin to make better choices for herself and her future.

You might be fearful that after speaking your truth, people will not support you or sympathize with your plight. And let's be honest, not everyone will. When Lisa finally got up the courage to admit to her impostor syndrome and what was going on for her, several people were quite harsh and suggested that she was creating the paralysis for herself and she just needed to get over it. But a significant group of people were supportive, compassionate, and gave very thoughtful suggestions. They also offered contacts and information about other opportunities. Many of those people are still members of Lisa's Dream Team (we'll discuss how to make your own in Step 8).

You will be surprised to find out that even if your loved ones, friends, and colleagues don't fully understand your experience, they will want to help you overcome the unhappiness and discomfort you are holding in. Your journey in addressing impostor syndrome thoughts and feelings must involve articulating them, admitting to them, and owning them in a public manner, which will diminish their power over you. The following activity asks you to identify two people in your life with whom you can share your impostor syndrome experience, including your triggers. Once you have named them, set a deadline as to when you will discuss your impostor syndrome with them.

TWO IMPOSTOR SYNDROME CONFIDANTS

Write the names of two trusted friends or family members that you can share some of your Impostor Syndrome experiences with that currently do not know that you are experiencing this. Share with them a description of what you are experiencing with your IS and some of your triggers and let them know that you are working on addressing your IS.

NAME

ACCOMPLISHMENTS

Another aspect of speaking your truth is recognizing and owning your accomplishments and strengths. You may believe that an accomplishment should be a major achievement, such as winning a Nobel Prize, founding your own company, or being a valedictorian. Therefore, you may tend to minimize or dismiss your hard-earned successes. We often work to teach our clients battling impostor syndrome to value their accomplishments and to be kind to and proud of themselves. An accomplishment is anything you can be proud of. This definition sometimes irks some people with impostor syndrome because they don't like when society rewards every little achievement and awards medals to everyone who participates. Thus, they struggle to identify what they deem to be an accomplishment because the bar is set extraordinarily high. However, no one is suggesting that everything you do requires a celebration, but for people with impostor syndrome, far more events require celebrating and recognizing than are currently being noticed. So, if you recently completed a major project or took a risk at work, those are accomplishments. Being named to an important committee or trying something new are accomplishments. Although you may feel resistant to the idea of naming accomplishments, speaking your truth also means acknowledging your efforts and their results, even if you have considered them minor in the past.

The experience of Cal demonstrates this struggle to speak one's truth, and how important it is to do so:

CASE STUDY: CAL

Cal was a vice president for a marketing firm. He sought executive coaching because he was struggling in his new role. He believed coaching could provide the boost he needed to be successful. Cal reported that he felt unable to speak up in key executive meetings and found it increasingly harder to make decisions when his direct reports asked him for guidance. He was extremely afraid to say the wrong thing or to make a mistake, which he believed would expose him as incapable of his senior-level role. During the course of the work with Cal, it was evident that he constantly experienced impostor feelings, which prevented him from settling into his new job. When he was asked to name some of his accomplishments in his life, he became tearful and stated that he didn't have any. We explored this disconnect by deconstructing and taking a deep dive into his experience. We ended up identifying several accomplishments, which he tended to overlook, like securing a multi-million-dollar account, being the youngest senior vice president in the history of his previous firm, and being recognized as a Rising Star by an industry trade publication.

Despite these accolades, Cal was convinced that he had no accomplishments of which to speak. Although it was initially very difficult for him to do so, Cal worked to identify more accomplishments, including graduating near the top of his college class, becoming a skilled violinist, and having several close friendships that spanned over 20 years. Once he was able to "speak his truth" by recognizing his accomplishments and his skills in achieving them, Cal's confidence grew, and he was able to internalize his successes and put his challenges in the appropriate context. He was no longer afraid to make decisions, and even if they didn't always go as planned, he felt confident enough to learn from the process and to continue making hard choices.

You may have the same struggles as Cal did in articulating your accomplishments. It may seem too boastful to do, or you may sincerely feel that you have not accomplished much up to this point in your life. While we recognize that it may not culturally feel comfortable for you to celebrate your achievements, it is a critical part of bolstering your confidence and overcoming your impostor syndrome. And we guarantee if you take a moment to do the deep dive like Cal did, you will find numerous accomplishments to cite.

OWNING YOUR ACCOMPLISHMENTS

Name three hidden accomplishments that you have not typically discussed, shared, or identified before. Describe the skills that you used to attain those accomplishments. If you feel stuck, ask a trusted family member or friend for some ideas to get you started.

1. Accomplishment:

_____

Skills to attain it:

_____

_____

2. Accomplishment:

_____

Skills to attain it:

_____

_____

3. Accomplishment:

_____

Skills to attain it:

_____

_____

STRENGTHS

Naming strengths is another area of discomfort for individuals with impostor syndrome. Take the case of Joel, a senior accountant who worked long hours and felt totally overwhelmed by his job. He sought out coaching to try to attain a better work-life balance, and to more effectively manage his team. Joel reported feeling underappreciated and constantly in fear of being terminated, even though he consistently earned strong performance reviews and bonuses. When we explored his strengths, Joel hesitated for a moment and stated, "Well, I think I am good with people. That's about it." After digging a little deeper, Joel was able to expand and to elaborate, discussing his problem-solving skills and leadership abilities.

Your narrative may be that you don't have any strengths and you have been fortunate to "get over" on people for so long as you advanced in your career. Therefore, when you are asked typical interview questions like, "What are your strengths?" you may feel deceptive or untruthful in providing an answer or struggle to come up with a viable response. We are always completely confident that when someone has impostor syndrome, they always have a slew of accomplishments, strengths, skills, and assets. No one with impostor syndrome lacks this. It's just a matter of teaching them how to see it.

Typically, those with impostor syndrome can easily identify strong interpersonal skills or analytical abilities, which they have often developed in service of hiding their need to work at things. In the Your Competencies Today exercise in Chapter 3, you learned having these skills is normal and typical of those who are capable. What about your other strengths? Are you able to stay calm in the face of a pressure-packed work environment? Are you skilled in meeting deadlines and delivering killer presentations? The activity at the end of this chapter will challenge you to identify in a greater and more exhaustive way your accomplishments and strengths. You may feel that at this point in the various exercises throughout the book you have listed as many strengths and accomplishments as you can. The point is for you to feel like you have a significant set of strengths to note. You will likely never feel stuck again when someone asks about your strengths. Remember, if you feel stuck, don't stay there, reach out to your trusted colleagues, friends, and family members to name some of your strengths and accomplishments. Again, you may be astounded by the information they provide.

If you struggle to identify your strengths, utilize Howard Gardner's concept of "multiple intelligences"[16] to start considering your strengths in a more robust way. This theory of multiple intelligences posits that people have many different ways of processing information that convey their intellect. Here are nine categories of intelligence that are studied within this model.

Gardner's Multiple Intelligences

Interpersonal	Understanding and interacting with others—communication, social skills, leadership, counseling, teaching
Intrapersonal	Detect and discern among one's own feelings, knowledge of self and ability to use that knowledge for personal understanding—reflection, critical analysis, self-motivation
Body-Kinesthetic	Coordination, motor skills and learn with hands-on activities—athletic, performing arts, trades and manual labor, outdoor pursuits, good reflexes, can handle objects skillfully, mind/body connection, taking things apart and putting them back together
Naturalistic	Understanding and connection to the natural world—identify plants and animals, enjoy the outdoors, value the environment, strong observational skills
Logical-Mathematical	Reasoning skills—solving problems using logical patterns—cause/effect, finding relationships and connections, scientific reasoning, IT, mathematics
Visual-Spatial	Perceiving the visual world accurately—to transform, manipulate and recreate images—drawing, grasp of color, form mental images from description, painting, designing, navigation and spatial orientation
Verbal-Linguistic	Using words effectively in writing and speech—persuasion, remembering information, explaining, public speaking, debating, reading, languages

---

16 Gardner, *Frames of Mind: The Theory of Multiple Intelligences.*

Musical-Rhythmic	Compose, perform and enjoy musical patterns, tones and rhythms, attentive to sounds in the environment—playing an instrument, singing, good auditory memory
Existential	Ponder and reflect on abstract theories about life and existence—meaning of life and death; experiences of love; connect present experiences to a bigger picture—intuitive, spiritualism, meditation

IDENTIFY THREE OF YOUR STRENGTHS

Identify three new strengths that have not been discussed before in another exercise. Next to the strength add the reason why you have dismissed this strength in the past.

1. _____

_____

_____

2. _____

_____

_____

3. _____

_____

_____

KEY TAKEAWAYS

- You recognize that staying silent about your impostor syndrome is not beneficial to overcoming it.

- You understand what "speaking your truth" means.

- You feel comfortable sharing your impostor syndrome experience with trusted others.

- You have awareness of and have begun to internalize your accomplishments and strengths.

- You identified persons with whom to share your impostor syndrome experience and have begun to share with them.

Chapter 6

STEP 5: SILENCE AUTOMATIC NEGATIVE THOUGHTS

The next component of Choose is silencing automatic negative thoughts (ANTs). When your impostor syndrome is fully activated, these thoughts immediately enter your mind, especially in unfamiliar or stressful situations. For instance, if you have to make a presentation to a group of colleagues for the first time, your automatic negative thought might be, "If I flub or use verbal fillers like 'um' or 'uh,' or if I get asked a question that I can't answer, they are all going to think I am stupid, unprepared, and won't take me seriously." These ANTs are intrusive and disruptive to your ability to think positively about yourself and to extinguish your impostor syndrome.

YOUR TYPICAL ANTs

Identify five of your typical ANTs below.

1. _____

2. _____

3. _____

4. _____

5. _____

Consider your impostor syndrome experience. How has it held you back in your life and career? Did it stop you from applying for a new job? Are you afraid to ask for a raise or a promotion because you don't believe you deserve it yet? Has it affected your performance because you lacked the confidence to produce your best work? Impostor syndrome can prevent you from living your best life possible due to the power of your negative thoughts, which support your theory that you are a fraud. It may also cause you to avoid opportunities due to fear of being exposed as incompetent.

Most individuals with impostor syndrome have automatic negative thoughts (ANTs). We like the acronym ANTs because it accurately coveys how these thoughts behave—they are like little tiny insects that creep into your mind and can carry a ton of weight if you let them. Automatic negative thoughts are beliefs, usually irrational, that immediately come to your consciousness when triggered, which serve to diminish your self-confidence and abilities. According to Leahy, Holland, and McGinn,[17] there are several types of ANTs for which you should be aware:

- **Mind-reading:** You believe you can interpret what other people are thinking about you. "Everyone thinks I'm an idiot."

- **Labeling:** You attribute negative character traits to yourself. "I am stupid and a fraud."

- **Fortune-telling:** You predict negative outcomes based on no evidence or faulty evidence. "I will be exposed as not being truly competent, if I try to find a new job."

- **Catastrophizing:** You consider the worst-case scenario when imagining outcomes. "I know I will be fired if I make a mistake."

- **Unfair Comparisons:** You set unfair or unrealistic standards by which to judge yourself. You compare yourself to others who you perceive are doing better than you, and consistently rate yourself as inferior to them. "Everyone here is so much smarter and accomplished than me. I don't really belong here."

- **Dichotomous (all-or-nothing) Thinking:** You engage in all-or-nothing thinking. "If I am not perfect, then I am a failure."

- **Discounting Positives:** You trivialize or diminish any positive feedback relative to your performance or character. "My supervisor gave me a compliment, but she didn't mean it, she was just being nice."

---

17   Leahy et al., *Treatment Plans and Interventions for Depression Anxiety Disorders.*

You may have experienced one or all of these ANTs, which supports your impostor syndrome and keeps you from having a more positive self-concept. When your impostor syndrome is fully activated, these ANTs can overwhelm you and make you feel stuck when trying to move forward in your life. Therefore, our goal is to silence these ANTs and to counter them with more affirming thoughts. This is known as "rational responding."

The key to silencing automatic negative thoughts is to first be aware of them in your daily lives. The activity below will enable you to identify the types of ANTs you experience and to provide examples of each. Once you are clear about your ANTs, the next step will be exploring how to counter and, eventually, silence them.

IDENTIFY YOUR ANTs

Name the types of ANTs you use to support your impostor syndrome, and give examples of each:

ANT: _____

Example: _____

ANT: _____

Example: _____

ANT: _____

Example: _____

ANT: _____

Example: _____

This example of Nadine shows how ANTs can impact your well-being:

Nadine was a first-year associate at a corporate law firm, who struggled with impostor syndrome. She excelled during her summer internship at her current firm during law school and was offered a full-time job. Nadine's typical ANTs were Unfair Comparisons, Fortune-telling, and Discounting Positives. During her internship, she would often think, "Everyone here is so smart and accomplished. I know that I am a hard worker, but I am so afraid that I will be found out for not being intelligent." When her supervisors gave her praise, she immediately thought, "They probably give the same compliments to all the other interns because they are just nice people."

Once she was hired as a full-time associate, Nadine sought career coaching assistance because she was having difficulty managing her impostor syndrome due to these overwhelming ANTs. She feared completing her work assignments, often turning them in late, because she thought, "Once they see all the errors that I am making, the firm will realize they made a mistake in hiring me, and I'll be fired." Unfortunately, the ANTs were impacting her performance, and further reinforcing her impostor syndrome.

Coaching with Nadine involved helping her identify these irrational beliefs as ANTs, and to identify each one. The next step was to help her silence them.

COUNTERING ANTs

Now that you have identified the types of ANTs you tend to utilize to sustain your impostor syndrome, it is time to discuss how to silence them. Silencing the ANTs requires that you counter them with more rational and affirmative thoughts. Although you may recognize that your ANTs are irrational, in the moment, they seem very real. Therefore, by going through the process of questioning and challenging the thought, you can diminish their power. For instance, if you have a Catastrophizing ANT that you made a horrible presentation and you were going to be fired as a result, challenging the ANT would entail asking some critical questions such as:

What is the evidence for and against the thought that the presentation was horrible? What did people do or say that verified this?

What would lead to me being fired as a result of this presentation? Have people been fired in the past for a single poor presentation? What was the process?

Examples of Challenging Questions for ANTs

FORTUNE-TELLING
- What evidence leads me to make such a negative prediction?
- When was the last time such a negative prediction came true?
- Would my friends and family make a similar prediction? Why or why not?

LABELING
- What is the data to support such a label?
- What is the cost or benefit of labeling myself so negatively?

DISCOUNTING POSITIVES
- What is the cost or benefit to me of invalidating such positive data?
- What makes it difficult for me to accept such complimentary feedback?
- What would be the gain for the person to give me a compliment, if he did not mean it?

MIND-READING
- What is the data to support my interpretation of what someone is thinking of me?
- What leads me to have such a negative conclusion about what someone is thinking about me?

UNFAIR COMPARISONS
- How appropriate is it to compare myself to this person?
- What might make such a comparison unfair or inaccurate?

DICHOTOMOUS THINKING
- What evidence leads me to think in these extremes?
- If I am not perfect, am I truly a fraud? Are there other ways to look at the situation? Are there shades of gray that I should consider? If so, what are they?

CATASTROPHIZING
- What is the evidence for and against the thought that the presentation was horrible? What did people do or say that verified this?
- What would lead to me being fired as a result of this presentation? When have people been fired in the past a result of single poor presentation? What was the process?

These questions challenge the validity of your ANTs and force you to consider a more rational conclusion for your experience, which is usually that your impostor syndrome is heightened. The following activity asks you to identify critical questions to challenge each type of ANT you may have.

OWN YOUR GREATNESS

CHALLENGING YOUR ANTs

Identify the ANTs that you experience most often and create two questions to challenge these ANTs.

_____

_____

_____

_____

_____

_____

_____

_____

_____

● ● ●

In addition to using challenging questions to counter your ANTs, another strategy is to replace them with more positive statements. For instance, if you tend to have Dichotomous Thinking, you should replace the ANT with a statement such as, "I did a great job on that project, and I deserve the praise I received." If you tend to have Mind-reading ANTs, you can counter them with a message such as, "My colleagues are not just being nice, they actually believe that I am competent and intelligent." If you often have Fortune-telling ANTs, you can amplify more positive thoughts such as, "If the project doesn't come out perfectly, I won't look like I have no clue what I am doing. I will just note what I need to do better next time." It is like raising the volume on the positive thoughts while lowering the volume on the ANTs. The goal is to make the positive thoughts as automatic as your ANTs so that, eventually, they become your default response. The activity below asks you to identify more positive statements for each of the typical ANTs you experience.

TURNING DOWN THE ANTs VOLUME

Now, take the ANTs from the previous exercise and provide at least one positive statement for each ANT.

• • •

During the course of the work with Nadine, we began to focus on how to silence these ANTs in order for her to bolster her self-confidence, thrive in her role, and reduce her fear and anxiety. Once we identified her common ANTs (e.g., Unfair Comparisons, Fortune-telling, and Discounting Positives), we then explored how to silence them.

If she wanted to automatically go to an Unfair Comparison, we would discuss replacing it with a more affirming response such as, "As a first-year associate, it is alright to have a question about a brief. It is normal for someone at this stage of my career to not have all the answers, or to know less than my more advanced colleagues." If she moved to use Fortune-telling as her ANT, we replaced it with the more positive statement, "I won't be fired if I make a mistake. I will get feedback, which will help me to grow and learn." Finally, if Nadine tried to go to her familiar Discounting Positives stance, I advocated for her to instead respond with, "I received and can take in that praise from my boss because I truly earned it."

The key to silencing ANTs is to consistently practice the positive statements by having an intention to do so every day. Say them out loud to yourself in front of a mirror, think about them on your way to work, or maybe even talk them through with your best friend or partner. The crucial part of this process is making a commitment to set aside time to do so every day, in order to make it as automatic as the ANTs have been. In an interview for the *Chronicle of Higher Education*,[18] Dean Valerie Sheares Ashby, who asserted that she had impostor syndrome until she was 43 (she was 51 at the time of the interview), discussed the notion of

---

18   Gluckman, "How a Dean Got Over Impostor Syndrome."

changing the negative tape in her mind, which freed her from impostor feelings. The goal of silencing the ANTs is to change the negative tape into a positive, uplifting one.

Nadine made a commitment to practice her positive statements every morning before work, saying them out loud in front of her mirror. Although she initially felt silly doing so, after regular practice, Nadine felt more comfortable and fully embraced the exercise. Over time, she was able to internalize these positive statements.

The activity below asks you to discuss your plan for practicing your positive statements, including how (e.g., saying it out loud) and when (e.g., before, during, or after work, before bedtime) you will do so.

YOUR POSITIVE TAPE PLAN

Write down your commitment to practice the positive rational responses to your ANT. Note when you will practice them and how you will practice them (e.g., in front of the mirror, with my partner).

I commit to practicing my positive rational responses…

_____

_____

_____

_____

_____

_____

_____

- You recognize how automatic negative thoughts (ANTs) sustain your impostor syndrome.

- You identified the types of ANTs you typically utilize.

- You understand how to silence the ANTs through challenging questions and replacing them with positive statements.

- You have made a commitment to practicing your positive statements consistently and developed a plan to do so.

Chapter 7

STEP 6: VALUE YOUR SELF-CARE

The final component of Choose is valuing your self-care. You may find it very challenging to take care of yourself because your impostor syndrome convinces you that you must work to the point of exhaustion in order to prove that you are worthy of your job. Therefore, individuals with impostor syndrome tend to be at risk for burnout and other stress-related issues. Chapter 7 will explore critical strategies for you to place your self-care at the forefront of your efforts, such as integrating it into your day-to-day practice, to defeat impostor syndrome. Such self-care also includes setting appropriate boundaries at work and in your personal relationships, and having an accountability partner to support your self-care goals.

Overworking and perfectionism are hallmarks of impostor syndrome. Overworking attempts to compensate for the fear of being exposed as a fraud, but it can easily lead to exhaustion and burnout. Perfectionism strives toward unrealistic expectations that are impossible to maintain and sets unattainable goals that reinforce the experience of failure. Hopefully, by this point through your work with the book, you realize that these methods don't really work to alleviate the impostor feelings, but just leave you totally spent. In fact, they can leave you feeling more like a fraud. This chapter will examine strategies for you to put your self-care first, to avoid the burnout and overworking trap, and to contend with perfectionism. We will discuss the signs of impostor syndrome–induced burnout and will explore how to ensure you are consistently focused on your physical, mental, and emotional well-being, on the road to conquering impostor syndrome.

IMPOSTOR SYNDROME—INDUCED BURNOUT

The following case of Dennis illustrates the impact of impostor syndrome induced burnout on one's functioning:

Dennis was an assistant professor of psychology on the tenure track, who was having difficulty managing his impostor syndrome and its consequences. He decided to seek coaching because he felt extremely burned out. Dennis reported constantly overworking, coming into the office hours before his colleagues and usually being the last to leave. During our initial session, he discussed feeling that he was not smart enough to compete with his colleagues. He asserted that his only competitive advantage was to work harder than everyone else. Although this drive and philosophy seemed to work in graduate school, he now found that it left him feeling increasingly overwhelmed and tired in his workplace. He thought about work incessantly, even on the weekends. Dennis felt unable to relax, was constantly fatigued, and dreaded going to work. These were all signs of burnout.

During his first session, we discussed the symptoms of burnout with Dennis, and the connection surprised him. Dennis thought that you needed to be at a job for several years before you could experience burnout. We talked about the fact that it wasn't the duration of one's time at a workplace, but the intensity of the experience and a lack of self-care, which can contribute to burnout.

DEFINING BURNOUT

Although the term "burnout" is often used to describe one's feelings about work, it is important to define it for the purposes of discussing it within the context of impostor syndrome. The World Health Organization (WHO) recently included burnout in its International Classification of Diseases (ICD-11) as an occupational phenomenon, not a medical condition. The WHO defines it as follows:

> "Burnout is a syndrome conceptualized as resulting from chronic workplace stress that has not been successfully managed. It is characterized by three dimensions:
>
> • Feelings of energy depletion or exhaustion;
>
> • Increased mental distance from one's job, or feelings of negativism or cynicism related to one's job; and
>
> • Reduced professional efficacy.

Burnout refers specifically to phenomena in the occupational context and should not be applied to describe experiences in other areas of life."

While burnout is not considered a disease by this classification, it is viewed as a factor influencing health status and the need to engage with health-care providers. According to a recent Gallup study, 23 percent of employees reported feeling burned out at work very often or always, and an additional 44 percent reported feeling burned out sometimes. Therefore, it is evident that a significant number of people experience burnout at work.

Typical Burnout Signs and Symptoms

In addition to fatigue, constant dread about work, and an inability to relax, some other typical signs of burnout are withdrawal or disengagement at work, irritability, apathy, difficulty sleeping, anxiety, and feeling hopeless or helpless about your circumstances. These symptoms are generally related mostly to work, rather than a more generalized focus, which distinguishes it from other mental health concerns such as depression.

Do you start feeling a sense of distress on the weekend in anticipation of Monday and a job that seems to feed your insecurities? Do you feel a lack of motivation for a job that feels like it's not fully utilizing your talents, skills, and education? Is it difficult for you to even considering leaving because a job search feels like an overwhelming burden and you still want to prove yourself? Are you exhausted because you are working 10- to 12-hour days and everyone else is working 8 hours? Then, you may be experiencing burnout caused by impostor syndrome.

BURNOUT ASSESSMENT

Name the signs and symptoms of burnout/stress you are currently experiencing.

_____

_____

_____

_____

_____

SETTING SUITABLE BOUNDARIES TO COMBAT BURNOUT

The messages that we receive from our environment that reward overworking and not setting appropriate boundaries can be a major challenge to valuing yourself. We are expected to respond to e-mails from our bosses at all hours. We are often expected to forego scheduled plans if something comes up at work. We have to ask weeks and months in advance for time off, and it's possible for it to be denied. Our parental leave policies are often pathetically little, as compared with other places in the world.

When your impostor syndrome takes hold, your tendency to overwork and to burn out increase exponentially, as does your desire to please others. Therefore, when you are asked to complete additional projects, volunteer for a work group, or help a colleague with an assignment, it is difficult for you to set suitable boundaries and to sometimes say "no" to show that you belong and are capable.

Returning to the case of Dennis, you can see the practical challenges of setting appropriate boundaries at work. Dennis knew logically that he needed to reduce his work hours and to focus on his self-care, but at times, he felt unable to control the urge to put in 12-hour days. This resulted in him saying "yes" to several committees and editorial boards. He now felt that he was drowning in commitments, with no way out. Once we established the value of self-care and developed a plan for him to do so, our work with Dennis shifted to helping him to create appropriate boundaries in his life. We discussed setting limits on his work schedule and prioritizing the number of work responsibilities he pursued.

We set a reasonable work schedule, with identified start times and end times, and created a priority list of responsibilities. With these tools, Dennis was able to reduce his burnout symptoms and regained a healthier relationship with his job.

The following activities ask you to consider how your external environment is impacting feelings of impostor syndrome—induced burnout or stress, and how you can create strategies to set appropriate boundaries to protect yourself.

CONTRIBUTORS TO YOUR BURNOUT

Describe how your external environment (e.g., boss, supervisor, work culture, job duties, etc.) contributes to your impostor syndrome–induced burnout or stress.

_____

_____

_____

_____

_____

_____

_____

BOUNDARY-SETTING STRATEGIES

Identify your strategy to set ONE appropriate boundary at work and in your personal life. This could include setting your ideal schedule with start and end times for work, and other self-care activities (e.g., exercise, sleep, etc.)

Work boundary:

_____

_____

_____

_____

_____

Personal life boundary:

_____

_____

_____

_____

• • •

VALUING YOURSELF: ROLE CLARITY AND EVALUATION

A lack of role clarity and an unclear understanding of your work performance can also contribute to impostor syndrome–induced burnout. As a faculty member, Dennis did not have a direct supervisor. Although his chairperson and his more senior colleagues could provide some guidance about how he should approach his job, they were not as helpful in clearly illuminating the key aspects of his role to achieve tenure, or his progress in meeting them. This led to Dennis feeling overwhelmed and unsure about what his priorities should be, resulting in burnout. When you are not clear about the parameters of your role, you can have difficulty understanding how you are performing and what you should prioritize. For someone experiencing impostor syndrome, this can result in overworking, in an attempt to meet unrealistic and unfair expectations. Therefore, it is critical that you are able to clarify your role expectations and to understand your progress in meeting them. Individuals experiencing impostor syndrome can be fearful of having such a discussion because they believe they will be exposed as a fraud for even raising it. Prepare for it by having thoughtful, open communication with a coach or mentor in your field (as we will discuss in Chapter 9) around the areas that need clarification. It can be quite productive and reduce your impostor syndrome–induced stress in the long-term.

Dennis was able to sit down with his chairperson to discuss the most important elements of his role, and to gain better insight about how he was performing and his road to tenure. This discussion relieved some of his impostor syndrome–induced stress and allowed him to set more realistic expectations for himself and his schedule. The following activity asks you to identify your strategy to clarify your role expectations and to explore your progress in meeting them (e.g., speaking to your supervisor, reviewing your updated job description, etc.).

CLARIFYING ROLE EXPECTATIONS

Identify any aspect of your current role that requires clarification (i.e., it is requiring to do additional work because you are unclear about expectations).

_____

_____

_____

_____

_____

_____

_____

_____

SELF-CARE: OVERCOMING BURNOUT

One of the keys to overcoming impostor syndrome–induced burnout is to be intentional about your self-care. Consider the activities that you view as pleasurable and stress-reducing. It might be yoga or going to the gym. It might be meditation or going for a nice, brisk run. Or it might be getting a massage or a facial once a month. Developing a commitment to these activities and scheduling them consistently will be critical to avoiding or addressing burnout.

It is important, however, to clarify that certain activities that may be enjoyable may not be useful for self-care. Activities that have a clear, negative cost are not self-care activities. For example, shopping can provide temporary relief. However, the negative cost can increase expenses and put pressure on your budget. Other examples might include binge eating, the use of alcohol and drugs, prolonged exposure to television and video games, and anything that has negative consequences.

Dennis knew that his burnout was wearing him down and that he needed to focus on his self-care activities. However, he felt that his impostor syndrome made it impossible for him to do so. It told him that if he didn't put in the time, he would fall behind, and that he didn't want to waste time on "leisure" activities, which would not help him secure tenure. Our work then focused on having him begin to understand the value of these self-care activities. He was then able to consistently schedule time to go to the gym three times a week, and made getting a monthly sports massage a routine part of his self-care plan.

PERFECTIONISM: A MAJOR BARRIER TO SELF-CARE

The example of Brandon demonstrates how perfectionism also serves as a barrier to self-care.

> *Brandon was a copy editor for a major magazine publisher. He came to counseling because he was experiencing heightened anxiety and panic attacks. During our initial consultation, Brandon reported that he recently started his job, after serving as a fact-checker for two years at a smaller publisher, right out of college. One of his college roommates, who was leaving the magazine publisher role, recommended him for the position. As he discussed his work life, Brandon expressed impostor feelings, coupled with perfectionistic tendencies. He didn't believe he deserved the role and was fearful that he would soon be exposed as being incapable of fulfilling his duties. Brandon recalled that his first panic attack occurred when he realized that he made a minor error on one of the articles being sent to press. He knew he needed to tell his boss but started to have shortness of breath and thought he was about to faint. After gathering himself outside for about 10 minutes, Brandon returned and informed his boss of his oversight. Although the boss took it in stride and the article was recalled before going out, Brandon spent the next several hours ruminating about it and beating himself up for the mistake. Counseling work with Brandon involved helping him to recognize how his impostor syndrome and his perfectionism worked hand in hand to sabotage his efforts at self-care and to increase his anxiety.*

Several studies have indicated a positive correlation between perfectionism and impostor syndrome.[19] Typically, individuals with impostor syndrome feel that they have no room to make mistakes, because if they do, it will finally reveal their incompetence and fraudulent identity. Rather than attending to their self-care, they are constantly striving to avoid any mistakes and are extremely upset when they make an error.

---

19   Dudau, 2014; Henning, Ey, and Shaw, 1998; Vergauwe et al., 2015.

TYPICAL PERFECTIONISTIC BEHAVIORS

It is impossible to avoid mistakes completely, but for a perfectionist, it emotionally feels like the only option for success and survival. Therefore, perfectionists tend to demonstrate the following behaviors:

- Constant rumination after making a mistake, which can interfere with sleep or other activities.

- Berating yourself verbally or with automatic negative thoughts for not being perfect.

- Setting unrealistic expectations and beating yourself up when you don't reach them.

- Always comparing yourself to others you regard as perfect.

- Punishing yourself for making mistakes by withholding pleasurable or stress-reducing activities (e.g., time with friends, going on a trip, etc.).

- Procrastinating or avoiding tasks because they must be perfect.

- Refusing to compromise or to collaborate if your perfect solution is not adopted.

Perfectionism in tandem with impostor syndrome creates self-care neglect, which adversely impacts career and life satisfaction. By understanding which perfectionistic behaviors you demonstrate, we can change your response to increase your focus on self-care.

HOW YOUR PERFECTIONISM FUNCTIONS

Describe all your typical perfectionistic behaviors and when they are usually triggered (e.g., at work when beginning a new task, with friends or family, etc.)

Perfectionistic behavior: _____

_____

Trigger: _____   _____

_____

_____

Perfectionistic behavior: _____

_____

Trigger: _____

_____

_____

Perfectionistic behavior: _____

_____

Trigger: _____

_____

_____

• • •

COMBATING PERFECTIONISM

Once Brandon reframed his mistakes as opportunities for learning and growth, he was able to combat his perfectionism, decrease his anxiety, and focus more on his self-care, resulting in a much-improved work situation. One of the factors that may make it extremely challenging to shift your mindset is your external environment. If you were raised in a family that demanded perfection or currently work in a job where your boss or colleagues do so, it might feel very threatening to fall short of that expectation. Or you may have been rewarded for being perfect, and you may be reluctant to lose that status. While we appreciate the difficulties of such realities, we also recognize that they are not healthy to your overall well-being. Thus, it will be essential for you to find supporters in your friend, family, or work networks who will remind you that your perfectionism is more harmful than helpful to your self-care and, ultimately, to your life satisfaction. To further combat your perfectionism and to shift your mindset, consider the following strategies:

• Focus on "good enough," not perfect. Perfectionists hate this notion of "good enough," because it signals to them a lack of effort to be perfect, or a decline in quality of performance or product. However, when you realize that "good enough" does not mean that the quality of your work will suffer, and will in fact allow you to deliver in a timely manner, you can become more productive.

- Recognize the perfectionism hurts you and those around you. Accepting that your quest for perfection is doing more harm than good can enable you to give it up.

- Be proud and accepting of your humanity. When we discuss self-care, we ask our clients to be kind to themselves, and accepting their humanity is a major step in doing so. Embrace the notion that you are attempting to get better each day, and give yourself much-deserved credit for doing so—not to make you complacent, as many perfectionists fear, but to keep you motivated and optimistic to reach your goals.

THE GROWTH MINDSET

Dr. Carol Dweck,[20] a psychologist, coined the terms "fixed mindset" and "growth mindset" to discuss how people feel about intelligence and learning. In her research, she noticed that some students seemed more devastated by a setback than others who were able to better persist and overcome failure. A person with a fixed mindset tends to believe that intelligence is finite and innate, and if you fail, it is evidence of your intellectual shortcomings. These individuals feel that effort on a task is futile, and if something doesn't come easy, then it is an indication of one's limited potential.

Those with a growth mindset, in contrast, believe that intelligence is not finite, and one can improve through effort and hard work. They recognize that failure is an opportunity for growth and learning, rather than a sign of one's lack of ability. Individuals who adopt a growth mindset approach learning with less stress and anxiety than one with a fixed mindset, and are less likely to have perfectionistic tendencies, since they value mistakes as a chance to learn.

An example of how adopting a growth mindset can help you overcome impostor syndrome is the situation where you might compare and despair, when using the ANT of Unfair Comparisons. Typically, in this situation, when you have a fixed mindset, you might feel jealousy, a sense of competition, or anger toward a colleague who you believe is perfect, and therefore, you avoid working with them. However, when you adopt a growth mindset, you might reach out to that person, seek to learn from them, collaborating rather than competing, and understanding the benefit of doing so for your own development.

---

20 Dweck, *Mindset.*

- Only compare yourself to you. It's easy to look around and to find others you believe are perfect and are doing better than you. However, it is often an unfair comparison, and one you will usually lose. Therefore, the goal should be to try to improve every day and to note your growth from one period to the next.

- Find comfort in choosing your own path. Be confident in your judgment and decision-making, to realize that you are headed in the right direction for your current life needs.

- Learn to accept the beauty of compromise. Recognizing that there isn't one perfect way to do things can allow you to be more collaborative and provides you space to have a variety of options at your disposal.

- Choose standards that feel reasonable. Set realistic expectations by asking trusted others for their opinion on what those might be, and work to reach them.

- Appreciate that mistakes provide opportunity for growth. Using a growth mindset means understanding that mistakes offer an opportunity to deepen knowledge and skills for your development.

- Realize that perfection is unattainable and reaching for it makes you feel like a failure. One of the hardest strategies is to actually give up perfectionism without it feeling like a defeat, but rather a victory for your long-term growth, success, and satisfaction.

HOW TO COMBAT PERFECTIONISM

Identify at least two strategies you will utilize to combat your perfectionism.

Strategy 1:

_____

_____

_____

_____

_____

Strategy 2:

_____

_____

_____

_____

_____

STRATEGIES FOR SELF-CARE

Many of our clients suffering from impostor syndrome tend to believe that self-care is not the answer, but rather working more and striving for perfection are the solution. We often explore the cost of impostor syndrome–induced burnout to illuminate the importance of focusing on their physical and emotional health. The previously mentioned Gallup study found employees experiencing burnout are 63 percent more likely to take a sick day, 23 percent more likely to visit a hospital emergency room, and 13 percent less confident about their performance. The combination of impostor syndrome and burnout can literally make you sick. Therefore, it is clear that focusing on self-care is not a luxury, but a necessity. Also, once you have experienced burnout, you are more likely to experience it again, and it tends to come on even more quickly the following times, which is why developing good self-care habits are critical for long-term health.

MICRO-HABITS

So, how do you emphasize self-care in your life to combat your impostor syndrome, perfectionism, overworking, and burnout? It is by being intentional and starting small through micro-habits. Micro-habits are actions that require minimal motivation or effort to complete. When we think about self-care goal-setting, you might immediately think big. For example, if you are currently not going to the gym or a yoga class, deciding that you will now go to the gym or yoga five times a week is likely too big of a leap to make this change achievable and sustainable. The first step is not even going to the gym or the yoga class. The first step is developing a micro-habit of simply packing your gym clothes or yoga mat at home and finding a day to start. The next micro-habit is to go to the gym one day a week consistently, then two days, and so on until you meet your five-day a week goal. By developing micro-habits for your self-care goals, you can deepen your commitment to them and strengthen your ability to achieve them.

TASK AND TIME MANAGEMENT: KEYS TO SELF-CARE

Clients often pinpoint lack of time as a major barrier to their self-care. "I wish I had time, but between work and taking care of the family, there just is no time" is a common refrain. Two of the strategies we recommend that our clients use to manage their time better, especially if they might be a procrastinator or a self-saboteur, are the Pomodoro technique[21] and time blocking.

The Pomodoro technique is based on the notion that although we often seek large blocks of time (e.g., three hours of dedicated focused time) to accomplish a task, it might be more useful and productive to break down tasks into 25-minute increments, or pomodoros (named after the tomato-shaped timer used to set the increments). For instance, if you would like to clean your room, you might believe that it will take about 2 hours to do so. Finding two solid hours may prove to be daunting, and you may decide to not even begin the process. However, if you break it down into pomodoro increments, you might be able to initially commit two pomodoros (50 minutes) to the task. The key is to do one pomodoro (25 minutes) of focused work, and take a five-minute break, and then do the next one. Breaking tasks into smaller increments might help you overcome your procrastination, and to get started.

Once you identify the tasks and assign pomodoros, we recommend that you now use time blocking to manage your time. Time blocking is a technique where you visually account for all your time during the course of any given day. Rather than use a to-do list, which doesn't typically have time periods attached to them, time blocking enables you to see what activities you are prioritizing, and the amount of time you spend on them. Therefore, a time block might look like the table on the next page:

---

21   Noteberg, *Pomodoro Technique Illustrated.*

	TUESDAY 16	WEDNESDAY 17	THURSDAY 18
9:00am to 10:00am	Inbox management 9am–9:30am Meeting with Joan 10:00am–11:00am	Inbox management 9am–9:30am Work on project proposal	Inbox management 9am–9:30am All hands staff meeting
11:00am to 12:00pm	Administrative work 11am–12pm	10am–11:30am Brief conference call check-in 11:30am–12pm	10am–11:30am

Once you time-block key activities (e.g., work, sleep, family time), you can then commit a time block to your self-care activities (e.g., one hour of yoga on Wednesday evenings, 30-minute training session on Thursday morning), making it a part of your day-to-day routine.

SELF-CARE ACTIVITIES

The most common question we hear when we raise self-care to clients struggling with impostor syndrome is, "What is self-care and where do I even start?" It can be incredibly hard to think about effective self-care activities when you have rarely, if ever, engaged these experiences and have often felt like these things are indulgent and a waste of time.

We often get our clients started with "The Schedule of Pleasant Events" (see list below). These are a set of self-care activities that are commonly used for rejuvenating and filling your tank with little or no negative consequences. The key is committing to trying new ones until you have a set that you know and are confident will replenish you. The reason you need a set is because some are harder to do in a particular moment than others. Sometimes you won't feel up to one, so you'll have to use another, and they will each give you different levels of benefit. Eventually, you will know exactly what you may need in a particular moment.

SCHEDULE OF PLEASANT EVENTS

1. Soaking in the bathtub
2. Collecting things (coins, shells, etc.)
3. Planning a vacation
4. Breathing exercises
5. Recycling old items
6. Going on a date
7. Meditating
8. Going to a movie

9. Exercise

10. Engaging in gratitude

11. Listening to music

12. Laughing

13. Thinking about my past trips

14. Listening to others

15. Reading magazines or newspapers

16. Hobbies (stamp collect-
    ing, model building)

17. Spending an evening with good friends

18. Planning a day's activities

19. Meeting new people

20. Remembering beautiful scenery

21. Repairing things

22. Remembering the words and
    deeds of loving people

23. Having a quiet evenings

24. Taking care of nature, plants, gardening

25. Hiking

26. Drawing

27. Journaling

28. Going to a party

29. Having discussions with friends

30. Having family get-togethers

31. Singing around the house

32. Arranging flowers

33. Practicing religion (going to
    church, group praying, etc.)

34. Going to the beach

35. A day with nothing to do

36. Going skating

37. Going boating

38. Doing arts and crafts

39. Taking a nap

40. Going for a drive

41. Entertaining

42. Going to clubs/groups (book club,
    Parents without Partners, etc.)

43. Singing with groups

44. Playing musical instruments

45. Making a gift for someone

46. Cooking

47. Writing short stories, nov-
    els, poems, or articles

48. Sightseeing

49. Early morning coffee and newspaper

50. Going to plays and concerts

51. Listening to podcasts

52. Going bike riding

53. Watching a spectator sport
    (football, hockey, baseball)

54. Playing with animals

55. Reading fiction

56. Acting

57. Spending time by yourself

58. Shooting pool

59. Going to museums

60. Thinking about my good qualities

61. Taking a sauna or a steam bath

62. Going bowling

63. Doing woodworking or carpentry

64. Taking dance classes

65. Debating

66. Sitting in a sidewalk café

67. Having an aquarium

68. Going horseback riding

69. Solving a problem, puzzle, or crossword

70. Shaving

71. Speaking or learning a foreign language

72. Designing or drafting

73. Reading professional literature

74. Going to a fair, carnival, circus, zoo, or amusement park

75. Planning or organizing something

76. Listening to the sounds of nature

77. Giving a speech or a lecture

78. Improving my health (eating healthy, going to the doctor)

79. Learning to do something new

80. Supporting causes you believe in (social, political, or environmental)

81. Going to the movies or renting one

82. Washing my hair

83. Doing experiments and other scientific work

84. Getting a massage

85. Taking adult education courses

86. Being in a support group

87. Doing housework or laundry

88. Amusing people

89. Going to a barber or hair stylist

90. Having houseguests

91. Sleeping late

92. Going to the library

93. Playing games

94. Writing cards or notes

95. Talking about my hobbies or special interests

96. Smiling at people

97. Going to auctions, garage sales, and so on

98. Doing volunteer work, working on community service projects

99. Water sports

100. Reading cartoons, comic strips, or comic books

MINDFULNESS

One of the self-care techniques we strongly recommend is mindfulness. Jon Kabat-Zinn, the founder of the Mindfulness-Based Stress Reduction program at the University of Massachusetts, defines mindfulness as "the awareness that arises through paying attention, on purpose, in the present moment, non-judgmentally, in the service of self-understanding and wisdom."

In our day-to-day hectic routines, we are so used to making quick decisions and judgments about everything we do. However, this rapid pace can increase our stress, leaving us exhausted, anxious, and filled with self-doubt.

Mindfulness can be cultivated through meditation and breathing techniques such as coherence breathing, a breathing technique that involves taking long slow breaths at a rate of five per minute. It has been demonstrated to reduce stress and calm the body through consistent practice.

SELF-CARE MICRO-HABITS

Identify one self-care goal from The Schedule of Pleasant Activities or one that you have come up with on your own and the micro-habits that you will develop to achieve it. Include a time frame.

SELF-CARE MICRO-HABITS

SELF-CARE ACTIVITY	MICRO-HABITS	TIME FRAME
	1.	
	2.	
	3.	
	4.	
	5.	

• • •

IDENTIFYING A SELF-CARE ACCOUNTABILITY PARTNER

While we may all have good intentions, we all need a nudge sometimes to facilitate our goal achievement. As you develop your self-care action plan, it will be important for you to identify an accountability partner to support your progress. As the name suggests, an accountability partner is someone who can check in on you, to ensure that you remain on track in reaching your self-care goals. If your plan is to go to a yoga class twice a week, you might ask your accountability partner to send you a text once a week to find out how that goal is proceeding. The key part of identifying an accountability partner is that it should be a person with whom you have a trusting relationship and to whom you would respond. It will not be productive to have an accountability partner who doesn't follow through, whom you feel you can easily ignore or be unresponsive to, or to whose support you would respond negatively. Once you find your accountability partner, it will be critical for you to discuss your self-care goals with them, as well as the frequency (weekly, daily, etc.) and method (e.g., text, phone call, e-mail, etc.) you would prefer that they reach out to you. The following activity helps you get started identifying an accountability partner.

SELF-CARE ACCOUNTABILITY PARTNER

Identify your accountability partner. How often do you want them to reach out to you? What method do you want them to use to reach out to you?

_____

_____

_____

• • •

SOLIDIFYING SELF-CARE

Once you have created your self-care goals and identified your accountability partner, the last step in integrating self-care into your daily life is to post a visual reminder about its importance. The simple act of writing down a reminder, booking it into your calendar, and posting it where you can see it (e.g., refrigerator, bedroom mirror, phone, etc.) can improve motivation and goal completion.

MAKING SELF-CARE PLANS VISIBLE

What is the most reliable way to make your self-care intentions visible for yourself? Once you have identified your strategy to do so (e.g., posting it on your refrigerator, putting it in phone), create a reminder for your new self-care activity and micro-habits.

KEY TAKEAWAYS

- You recognize your signs and symptoms of impostor syndrome–induced burnout or stress.

- You identified strategies to set suitable boundaries in your work and personal life.

- You clarified your role expectations to reduce your impostor syndrome–induced stress or burnout.

- You recognize how your perfectionism contributes to self-care neglect.

- You identified your perfectionistic behaviors and strategies to counter them.

- You learned how adopting a growth mindset can reduce perfectionistic tendencies.

- You developed a self-care plan and goals, including micro-habits to increase your ability to achieve them.

- You created a reminder about the importance of self-care in reducing impostor syndrome–induced burnout and stress and posted it in a visible place.

- You identified an accountability partner to support your self-care efforts.

PHASE THREE
CREATE

Chapter 8

STEP 7: EXPERIMENT WITH NEW ROLES

The third and final C of the 3 C's strategy is Create. It focuses on developing a new reality for yourself by experimenting with different roles, building your Dream Team of supporters and mentors, and understanding and creating the conditions for your optimal performance.

Experimenting with new roles involves giving up the roles which may exacerbate and sustain your impostor syndrome. Many people with impostor syndrome, for instance, are used to being helpers—often the "go-to" person in their work environment, with their friends, and in their family circle. They also rarely ask for assistance, due to their fear of being found out as not having all the answers, and thus, confirming their identity as a fraud. By experimenting with new roles such as seeking support, you can realize that no one will judge you negatively for not being perfect, and that it is acceptable to allow others to help you.

This chapter will discuss how to explore new roles at work and in your relationships, and how your impostor syndrome keeps you stuck in the same old roles, which do not allow you to advance in your career and in your personal life. The chapter will also explore the barriers that prevent you from taking on different roles and the strategies to transition into new roles, which will benefit you in the long term.

The case of Jeanine shows the need to take on new roles to overcome your impostor syndrome:

Jeanine was a very successful but unhappy corporate recruiter. She was the go-to person in her family and friend circle. Everyone called her when they needed career or life advice, emotional support, or money, and she very often obliged. But it was exhausting. Jeanine constantly felt tired and that she did not have enough time for herself during her daily routine. She would work 9 to 10 hours and would often be on the phone with friends for 1 to 2 hours each night, helping them through some of their current work or life challenges. Jeanine sought counseling because she was unsure of her career path and felt overwhelmed about making such a decision on her own.

As Jeanine discussed her current situation during our initial consultation session, she was asked whom she would usually seek out for advice or support. She paused for a moment, and then said, "To be honest, I really try to figure things out on my own. I don't really think the people in my life can help me out. They have their own problems, which I am always helping them through." It was clear that the Helper role did not go both ways in Jeanine's relationships. As our work progressed, we discovered that Jeanine's impostor syndrome contributed to her taking on the Helper role and feeling like she could not be helped. During one session, when we talked about the importance of seeking support from others, Jeanine replied, "Well, what would my friends and coworkers think about me if I asked them for help? I am afraid that they would see that I don't have it all together, and that how dare I act like I do." We talked about how this belief was really her impostor syndrome talking to her in an unproductive manner. Jeanine was able to recognize that asking for help would not cause her to lose her treasured status as a go-to problem-solver. Rather, it might actually enhance her image as someone who was always making an effort to grow, and that others would actually appreciate the opportunity to give back to her, for all the support that she provided them. Jeanine slowly began to seek assistance from her coworkers, her family, and her friends, and although it was initially very uncomfortable to do so, she became very grateful for their support.

Your impostor syndrome can convince you that to keep from being exposed as a fraud, you must only take up certain roles, which locks you into a very limited dynamic in your work and personal relationships.

TYPICAL ROLES FOR IMPOSTOR SYNDROME

Individuals with impostor syndrome tend to take up the following typical roles:

The Helper: Everyone reaches out to you when they have a problem. Sometimes, you are an expert in a particular type of problem solving (e.g., you are considered the bank or the shoulder to cry on). Sometimes, you are considered the expert at all problems. The issue with this role is that often when you are the Helper, no one ever thinks that you might need help. So, your needs largely go unrecognized.

The Superperson: Due to your heightened concern about being exposed as a fraud, you may be reluctant to collaborate and instead enjoy your role as a very successful individual contributor. While such a stance may allow you to excel individually, it may adversely impact the impression you make as a team player.

The Failure Avoider: To preserve what you believe to be a fraudulent identity as a very competent professional, you are very resistant to taking risks that might result in failure. Therefore, you might tend to avoid taking big chances with your career or in your job, such as pursuing a better opportunity, asking for a raise, taking a stretch assignment, or starting a business, which might take your career to the next level but has the possibility of failure. You might not take risks in your personal life, which results in narrowing your options, by avoiding opportunities for growth.

The Knowledge Hub: Being knowledgeable about a particular topic can allow you to briefly ward off the impostor feelings you typically experience and, therefore, you tend to want to share this knowledge. However, despite this knowledge, you rarely view yourself as an expert because you always fear that someone will know more than you. Therefore, you may live in constant anxiety of being asked a question that you will be unable to answer. As such, you may limit with whom (e.g., you may have a preference for dealing with laterals at your same level or junior team members) and where you share your knowledge (e.g., in one-on-one meetings or small groups), which doesn't enable more senior stakeholders to understand your value.

In your personal life, this can lead to people feeling that they can go to you for problems because you have knowledge in important areas. However, you can also be perceived as a know-it-all, which can sometimes prompt negative reactions to your knowledge sharing.

The Behind-the-Scenes Leader: Oftentimes, your impostor syndrome prevents you from being out in front and visible, either by speaking up in meetings or taking a role that is much more public facing. It feels safer for you to make your impact behind the scenes, in a more low-key manner. However, while your colleagues and supervisor may appreciate this style of leadership, such a position may not provide the type of exposure and credit needed for you to gain the notice, which would elevate your career. It also sometimes allows others to take credit for work that you have usually done, which can result in those around you being elevated due to work for which you are responsible. This can create resentment and frustration.

You may recognize yourself in some or all of these roles, which your impostor syndrome influences you to take on. Overcoming your impostor syndrome will require you to take on different roles, although it might be very uncomfortable to do so at first. Diversifying your roles with others allows you to perceive yourself in more complex ways, and those around you also have to follow suit.

NAME YOUR IMPOSTOR ROLES

Identify the types of roles that you are more likely to play as a result of your impostor syndrome.

1. _____

_____

2. _____

_____

3. _____

_____

• • •

THE COST OF CHANGING ROLES

While Jeanine initially recognized that holding on to the Helper role did not benefit her in the long term, she was very resistant to experimenting with new roles. She was reluctant to step out of her comfort zone and increasingly anxious about finally being found out as a fraud and as incompetent. Role changing really triggered this feeling. You may have some of the same concerns and don't feel that it will be worth the effort to experiment and adopt new roles. Your fixed role(s) can be very protective because they allow you to feel like an expert in particular domains. As a result, you may feel that the cost of doing so is not worth the potential outcome. It's common to fear losing social status or power in your work or personal relationships when you try new roles. Or worse, due to your impostor syndrome, you may be terrified that taking on a new role will result in full exposure of your lack of ability and identity as a fraud.

If you think that the benefits of the behavioral change do not outweigh the perceived costs, you won't make the change. This is why being clear about the benefits of taking on new roles is so critical.

ROLE COST-BENEFIT ANALYSIS

List at least two costs (e.g., exposure of your identity as a fraud, disappointment from others, heightened anxiety, etc.) and two benefits (e.g., career advancement; stronger, more layered relationships, increased confidence, less stress, etc.) of the roles that you currently take on.

ROLE COST-BENEFIT ANALYSIS

ROLE	COST	BENEFIT
	1.	1.
	2.	2.
	1.	1.
	2.	2.
	1.	1.
	2.	2.

EXPERIMENTING WITH NEW ROLES: COMMON OPTIONS

As you consider experimenting with new roles, you may be contemplating what some of those roles might be. Clearly, those roles are a 180-degree shift from the ones that you held. We are not suggesting that you can never take up the previous roles. We just encourage you to sprinkle your experience with some of these other roles. It will be beneficial to your growth to try new roles and be able to stretch yourself. Some of the common new roles for an individual with impostor syndrome to explore are:

The Help-Seeker: Rather than being the one with all the answers and the best advice, seeking the assistance from friends, family members, and colleagues when you are struggling can be beneficial.

The Risk-Taker: Instead of always playing it safe, you may want to expand your reach and attempt to take some calculated risks. We are not suggesting thoughtless, risky behavior. We are promoting, for example, taking on a project or task that is not a guaranteed slam dunk and could even result in failure. Failure, like success, is a skill. In order to fail well, you have to learn how to do it over and over again. While no one enjoys failing, learning from the experience can provide valuable insight about how to improve your performance in particular domains, which may be critical to your professional or personal development. As was discussed earlier in the book, adopting a growth mindset means that you will view failure as more of an opportunity to learn rather than as a permanent indictment of your ability and potential.

The Collaborator: Although you likely treasure your position as a significant individual contributor, trying on a new role as a group collaborator can expand your influence and deepen your relationships with other work colleagues. It can teach you new skills around team development and cohesion. It can also help you to build allies.

The Knowledge-Receiver: It can feel very powerful to hold the position of the person with all the knowledge and expertise. However, it can be very limiting to your professional and personal development because you may not be motivated to learn in areas unfamiliar to you. By admitting your knowledge gaps and being open to expanding your areas of expertise, you can broaden your influence and engagement, both at work and in your personal relationships. People like sharing their expertise, and it can be a bonding experience for someone to share their skills with you.

The Visible Leader: Your behind-the-scenes achievements may have served you well in the past, but by taking on a more visible position, either by speaking up more in meetings or agreeing to participate in more public-facing, high-profile assignments, you may be able to accelerate your career advancement and professional development.

NEW ROLE PLAY

Describe at least two new roles that you want to try at work and in personal relationships (list as many as you want to).

_____

_____

_____

_____

_____

• • •

EXPERIMENTING WITH NEW ROLES: LOW-STAKES ENGAGEMENT

Once you consider experimenting with new roles, first plan for a more low-stakes engagement, usually with trusted friends, colleagues, and family members. It will allow a safe space to try out these roles without an extreme level of discomfort or anxiety. For instance, if you are typically the Helper, you might become the Help-Seeker, asking your friends or family members for advice or support with a minor problem at work or in your personal life. Be prepared for these first attempts to feel awkward, since both you and your friend or family member might be used to your more traditional role. It may take some time to adjust to your new one. It may take several attempts and patience to comfortably settle into the new role.

Jeanine tried out the Help-Seeker role with her best friend, Gina. She had a problem at work and decided that instead of trying to work it out on her own, she wanted another person's perspective. Although she was scared that Gina might think she was not competent enough to deal with what Jeanine considered a silly work concern, with the support of our coaching work, she became committed to discussing it with her. During one of their regular brunch outings, she raised her dilemma. At first, Gina was surprised and wasn't sure how to respond, since Jeanine never indicated that she had any difficulties at work. However, once she realized how hard it must have been for her to share a concern, Gina was able to provide a viewpoint, which Jeanine had never considered. Jeanine felt a rush of relief and gratitude and thanked Gina enthusiastically with a big hug. During our coaching session, Jeanine talked about how powerful and liberating it was for her to admit that she didn't have all the answers, and to be able to accept Gina's assistance. She also shared that she even felt a little closer to Gina after the experience.

TRY ON THE NEW ROLE

Now that we have discussed experimenting with new roles in low stakes engagements, identify one person with whom you intend to try out a new role and visualize and describe your ideal, successful conversation with that individual.

• • •

EXPERIMENTING WITH NEW ROLES: HIGH-STAKES ENGAGEMENT

By now, you have created a plan to experiment with new roles in low-stakes situations. You have a template to try out the new role with a specific person you identified. It's time to explore how to move to more high-stakes engagements, especially at work.

Once Jeanine had the courage to adopt a new role with her friend Gina, we then discussed how she could transition to doing so at her job, which felt like a higher-stakes situation. Jeanine immediately indicated that she wanted to be a more Visible Leader with her executive team, especially during high-profile meetings. We developed a plan of action, where Jeanine could adopt this role by first engaging with key executive team members one on one using the low-stakes rule first. She asked for several meetings and was able to talk about her goals and achievements at the firm with them. Although she is introverted by nature, these one-on-one meetings allowed Jeanine to speak up a bit more about her accomplishments and allowed her executive team members to get to know her a bit better. After these engagements, Jeanine reported feeling much more comfortable voicing her opinions and felt that she gained influence, which benefited her career prospects.

When considering more high-stakes situations, it may be useful to think about incremental steps to achieving your goals. Becoming the Visible Leader, or the Risk-Taker might not happen overnight. It may take small steps that start as low stakes and incrementally gain importance to reach your desired outcome. The key is committing to your goal and planning those steps intentionally. Practice the skills with friends and family, and trusted others to continue to build the skills of those roles.

NEW ROLE ADOPTION PLAN

Now, that you have considered strategies to adopt new roles in higher-stakes situations, create your plan for doing so, including identifying the situation (e.g., work team, friend group, etc.), the role you would like to adopt (e.g., Visible Leader), the steps you will take to achieve this goal, and your time frame (e.g., in the next three months).

NEW ROLE ADOPTION PLAN

ROLE	SITUATION	STEPS	TIME FRAME
		1.	
		2.	
		3.	
		1.	
		2.	
		3.	
		1.	
		2.	
		3.	

• • •

CREATING A MORE EXPANSIVE MENU OF ROLE OPTIONS

Experimenting with new roles does not mean that you must give up your old roles. Being the Help-Seeker does not preclude you from also assisting others. Adopting a new role as the Risk-Taker does not mean that you should always be looking to stretch yourself and to take huge risks. Rather, taking on new roles can expand your repertoire of options, which can be utilized based on the situation. With these new roles in your arsenal, you can combat the components of your impostor syndrome that enforce rigidity, limited vulnerability, and lack of visibility. New roles can increase your sense of closeness with others, allow for new, unexpected opportunities for success, and expand your sense of yourself and what you are capable of in your personal and professional life.

KEY TAKEAWAYS

- You identified the different roles you typically play at work or in your personal life.

- You noted the costs and benefits of adopting these roles.

- You chose the new roles you wish to adopt at work and/or in your personal life.

- You developed a plan for both low- and high-stakes engagement in experimenting with these new roles.

- You are aware of how to bring new roles into the already existing roles that you have mastered, which has expanded your options.

Chapter 9

STEP 8: ESTABLISH YOUR DREAM TEAM

The next component of Create, establishing your Dream Team, builds on this idea of support by encouraging you to find mentors or coaches who can provide guidance, and, at times, a nudge, as you combat impostor syndrome. Individuals with impostor syndrome believe they should do things without help and are often reluctant to develop a community of supporters. This chapter will extensively discuss how to build this network, explore the misconception that one has to achieve "on my own" in order for any success to be legitimate and worthwhile, and affirm the role of this network in diminishing your impostor syndrome.

Throughout your impostor syndrome experience, you have likely struggled largely on your own. This classic feature of impostor syndrome makes it so intractable and difficult to eradicate. Its solitary nature and the shame that it often induces allow the impostor-related thoughts and behaviors that follow to thrive and feed upon themselves. This is why it is so incredibly important to build your Dream Team.

While this can seem like a straightforward task, it is often very difficult for people who are impacted by impostor syndrome for some central reasons. Identifying how these interpersonal concerns affect you and addressing them proactively become critical in building your Dream Team and maintaining them over time. The tendency to think you can do this alone can be strong and powerful, but it will work against you because the fear of vulnerability, being exposed, and being beyond help lurk underneath. Building these relationships around you to recover from your impostor syndrome gives you the opportunity to see that sharing vulnerability, flaws, and insecurities with the right set of people can make you stronger than you ever imagined in a real, authentic, and sustainable way. It can also deepen your relationships in surprising ways as the nature of those relationships shift along with your changing role.

In the last chapter, you started working on role shifts. You will continue that work here. Deep, healthy, long-lasting relationships require authenticity, honesty, vulnerability, and the ability to cope with growth and change. With the impostor persona, you don't often show some of these characteristics in a relationship because they threaten your fragile sense of self, but now you will. Not only will you be authentic, honest, vulnerable, and tolerant of your own growth, but you will find that seeing you in new and different ways encourages others to show different parts of themselves to you.

Through the example of Sandra, you can see how her impostor syndrome developed and how that closed family system prevented her from being vulnerable and tolerating mistakes:

> *Sandra is a 58-year-old woman who grew up the oldest of two children in tight-knit, protective family that was often suspicious of outsiders. Because her parents didn't come home from work until after 6 p.m., her few friends weren't allowed over. She wasn't able to go to other people's houses either.*

> *Sandra has struggled with her Impostor Syndrome since her college years. Her younger sister was considered the smart one and went to Ivy League schools for her undergraduate and graduate degrees. Sandra also attended really good schools and has made a great career for herself. However, she often gets triggered by impostor feelings when she makes a mistake or is behind in her work. She has found it really difficult to share these experiences with other people.*

> *Slowly, she is working on experimenting with new roles and taking risks to share vulnerable experiences with family members and those in her church. Lately, she has started to see that since she has begun to take those risks, people have been inviting her to more events and sharing with her. Sometimes this makes her feel suspicious of them or concerned that they will expect her to serve in roles she is trying to let go of, such as "the Helper," but she knows that this thinking comes from old messages that are not helpful to her. She is now more comfortable recognizing those feelings, observing them, and then choosing other supportive thoughts like "it takes a lot for*

someone to share," This has created a place for her to go when she feels triggered and has provided great comfort and relief.

Sandra's experience with attempting to develop her Dream Team is not uncommon. Through the course of having impostor syndrome, no doubt, you have either done much of the struggling alone and have potentially been reinforced in your environment to keep others from your experience. However, you need something very different now. You need a healthy crew of supporters. We say that because you don't need just anyone—you need specific types of people around you to be a part of that Dream Team. In fact, a recent study by Richard Gardner and his colleagues,[22] found that social support was one of the most important factors in dampening impostor feelings. Most significantly, the study indicated that finding individuals outside of one's peer competition group (e.g., friends, family, significant others) was the most powerful type of social support to help you overcome impostor syndrome.

CONSIDERING A THERAPIST

First, let us put in a plug for therapy. Sometimes, one of the most important members of your team, especially in the beginning when you are trying to establish healthy habits and skills, can be a licensed therapist. Finding a therapist can be a process. So, if you are new to this process, it might take some time to find the right fit. It's important to recognize that there are a variety of possible right fits, not just one person, so don't feel so much pressure to find "the one." Some things to consider in your search are:

- How much can you spend on therapy monthly? Will you need to use your insurance, or do you have out-of-network benefits? Can you consider private pay?

- In what geographical area do you want to be seen?

- What demographics of the therapist matter to you (e.g., gender, race, age, language spoken)?

- What expertise (e.g., anxiety, depression, relationships, career concerns) matters to you? Do culturally competent, specific types of treatment or training matter?

Create a document that outlines the specific aspects of a therapist that matter to you to help you get started. Then, you can use a national directory of licensed mental health professionals, like PsychologyToday.com, to begin your search. It's important to understand that many therapists are overloaded by calls from potential new clients so they may not answer the phone

---

22   Gardner et al., "I Must Have Slipped through the Cracks Somehow," 115.

immediately or at all. You may have to call a number of therapists to set up consultation calls (i.e., a short call for both the therapist and you to assess fit). In this call, share the issues that you want to work on in a succinct manner because these calls are often brief, about 10 to 15 minutes. You also want to ask questions that are relevant to you about how the clinician works or other important details. Make it clear to each therapist you set up initial meetings with that you are still looking for the right fit and speaking to more than one person. You shouldn't see multiple therapists for more than one or two sessions. After that, you will need to make a decision about who seems like the best fit. Again, any number of therapists can provide you with the support you need, and the decision doesn't have to feel like there is only one right choice.

FINDING A COACH

In addition to considering a therapist, another professional you can think about adding to your Dream Team is a career or an executive coach. Such a coach can help you manage some of your career or leadership concerns, especially as they are affected by your impostor syndrome. Unlike a licensed therapist, however, finding a coach can be more challenging, since it is not a licensed profession. Therefore, anyone can call himself or herself a coach, which makes obtaining quality assurance more difficult.

Generally, therapists are able to deal with longer-term, holistic concerns such as anxiety and trauma, while coaches tend to focus on shorter-term, specific issues such as career transitions and leadership development. However, as both licensed psychologists and executive coaches, we have the advantage of being able to address issues in a variety of personal and career domains. In fact, impostor syndrome is a great example of an issue that crosses psychological, career, and personal domains, and you will generally need a professional who can manage all these areas. Thus, we usually endorse finding a coach who has some level of mental health training (e.g., psychologists, mental health counselor, etc.), in addition to coaching experience.

RESOURCES TO FIND A COACH

Since quality assurance can be a concern when searching for a coach, it is important to utilize trusted resources to select one. Professional associations such as the National Career Development Association (NCDA) and the International Coach Federation (ICF) have coaching directories, with professionals who have demonstrated a level of competence to be included in the directory. In addition to professional associations, finding referrals from your personal or professional contacts may be another effective way for you to find the right coach for your needs. Similar to when considering a therapist, the following are questions to think about:

- How much can you commit to investing in coaching monthly?

- What are their qualifications?

- What expertise (e.g., career transitions, leadership, diversity, and inclusion issues) matters to you? Do culturally competent, specific types of training and work experience matter?

- In what geographical location do you want to be seen?

- What demographics of the coach are important to you (e.g., gender, race, age)?

Once you reach out to potential coaches, you want to make sure that you find a right fit. Feel free to ask questions about the coach's approach and the experiences he or she might have with clients who have similar concerns to yours. Even with a therapist and/or a coach, you will need additional members of your Dream Team because the therapist or coach is with you usually one to two hours maximum a week. The rest of the time you need a solid support network around you to sustain progress with healthy skills and habits.

OTHER DREAM TEAM MEMBERS

In addition to your therapist or coach, you will need a cadre of individuals who touch the important areas of your life that are impacted by your impostor syndrome. No one individual is going to serve as your everything. The following Dream Team members collectively support separate aspects of the fight to manage your impostor syndrome.

THE MENTOR

The mentor is a valuable and essential member of your team. It's actually important to have more than one because they can offer different perspectives and have different reach and access to provide as support. The qualities you should be looking for in a mentor are very closely related to the components of your impostor syndrome. Recent research suggests that it is more difficult for those who struggle with impostor syndrome to make connections in their field, which is likely due to the threat of exposing their "fraudulence" in a high-stakes environment. However, connecting with mentors from your field becomes critical to create protection from isolation, difficulty with advancement, and getting stuck in positions that reinforce the impostor syndrome. Given that this relationship may be difficult to cultivate at first, this perhaps may not be the first person that you work to find for your team. We will discuss a variety of other lower-stakes relationships that may support you to take the risks to reach out, develop, and build these mentoring relationships. Mentors are critical members of your team and cannot and should not be avoided.

So, what kinds of qualities does this mentor need to have? Obviously, the mentor should be senior to you in their accomplishments and successful in at least some aspects of their career, although they don't have to be at the top of their field in every single aspect. They should be genuinely interested in you and your career, and have some time to devote to connecting with you. You should feel like they are open and honest about their own struggles, missteps, and falls along the way. They should be good at providing constructive feedback, offering relationship connections, and helping you identify new opportunities. You should be able to share your difficult moments and feel like their response is grounding and provides you with some thoughtful ways to go back to the situation with a new point of view and, potentially, an action plan.

While it's amazing to find all of these qualities in one person, it is not likely that you will, which is why it is so important to have a variety of mentors so you can look to particular qualities in each person and connect with them when you need a particular strength from your mentor.

You can use this checklist to assess each of your mentors' qualities and be conscious of who you need to reach out to under different circumstances.

- ❏ Has significant career accomplishment; senior to you in experience or title
- ❏ Shows a genuine interest in your career
- ❏ Open and honest about their own struggles
- ❏ Gives constructive, usable, feedback
- ❏ Understands your competence and experience
- ❏ Identifies new opportunities for you
- ❏ Can share difficult moments with them
- ❏ Understands Impostor Syndrome and that you are working on addressing it

We preach reciprocity in all relationships. Our clients often struggle with how to do this in a mentoring relationship. While you are not likely going to provide career-advancement guidance to your mentor (although you'd be surprised, if your mentoring relationship lasts long enough, chances are you will get to the point where you will be providing this type of career guidance and support to them—trust us on that one), in the beginning, what you can provide is genuine interest—in them and in their lives. You can respect the gift of this relationship by always being on time for meetings, executing on advice (it doesn't have to be every piece of advice, but if you don't let them feel like they are impacting you, the mentoring relationship will fall apart), being grateful for what they offer, keeping them in the loop about what's going on in your life and career, and sharing articles, opportunities, and other information that might appeal to them. On an important note, generally people don't want to be asked to be your "mentor" because it can often imply a lot of work. Let these relationships develop with time, organically and naturally, but identify them to yourself as potential mentorships as you build your team. However, in some cases, you might be able to find a mentor through more formalized programs through alumni or professional industry associations, which may be useful if you are at a loss in identifying individuals who might be potential mentors.

While knowing the vital qualities necessary for a good mentor, you also want to beware of the qualities that make for a potentially toxic mentor. A mentor could have some of the positive qualities, but problematic qualities could nullify their usefulness. Some of the characteristics that you want to be on the lookout for are:

- Perfectionistic and controlling. They want everything executed in exactly the manner they suggest.

- Don't keep the confidences of others. Likely, they won't keep your disclosure in confidence either, which will threaten your overall trust.

- Support dysfunctional behaviors. They support behaviors like retaliation, avoidance, and cutting off any situation or person that causes distress. They support overwork as the means to success.

- Reactive and always self-referential. All their advice seems like it comes from a personal experience that is unresolved.

- Punitive (if you do something that they don't approve of or if they are disappointed with you).

- They always lack time, cancel on appointments, and don't follow through.

- They don't truly listen to you and are overly critical of everything you do.

After one experience of any of these behaviors, take note of it. If you start to consistently see these behaviors, consider moving on from having this person serve as a mentor for you.

THE CHEERLEADER

The Cheerleader serves an important role on your team as the person that you can rely on when you are feeling low and need a supportive boost. They believe in you unconditionally and know how to make you feel good pretty quickly. However, they may not have a lot concretely to give you in terms of feedback, suggestions, and planning. This is the person that you go to when you need a lift, emotional support, and general positivity. The trick for you will be to trust their responsiveness, not discounting it based on their relationship with you. For example, saying or thinking "they are only saying this because they love me. They don't know the real me" rejects the role that they serve on your team. Your job is to internalize the support and appreciate the lift so that you can engage other members of your team who will help support the other aspects of your recovery from your impostor syndrome.

THE GROUNDER

The Grounder is the person that you go to when you need the reality check. You reach out to them when you need to move away from irrational Catastrophizing toward rational responding. In the moment when you have made a mistake and think that as a result you are going to be fired or removed from a position of authority, this person is typically the one who helps you to frame the mistake in a way that makes it recoverable and appropriate to the situation. They help you to stop spinning. When working with the Grounder, the trick is to stop defending the position that you have committed the worst infraction, and to let them help you understand the true impact and how to begin to address it in a way that matches the actual mistake or error.

THE ACTION PLANNER

This person knows how to help you create a plan to respond to the impostor-triggered issue. They are usually someone who knows the lay of your professional land and can offer an informed position on what your options are. Unfortunately, a lot of people may feel like they are great Action Planners and want to offer you unsolicited advice. However, reliable people for this role are either very well-informed about the situation (they know the players, stakeholders, culture of environment) and/or have strong skills in interpersonal behaviors and the subject matter area or discipline and can provide useful suggestions. It's essential to have a variety of action planners around you because once you speak to them about the situation, you can pull thematic similarities from the conversations and find some sort of consensus about how you might proceed.

THE BIG-PICTURE PERSON

This person helps you put things into perspective and helps you see how the situation may or may not relate to your long-term goals and your future in general. The Big-Picture Person is very good at being able to help you understand how critical the issue is to the entire context of your life. To do this, they generally need to understand the various integral components of your life. They need to be trusted with personal aspects, such as the various communities that you belong to and find valuable, as well as some of the goals you have for these areas of your life. This can include family, social relationships (i.e., friends and romantic partners), religious community, hobbies, and future plans and priorities for your life.

THE IMPOSTOR EXPERT

This will likely be the hardest person to find for your Dream Team, and you may have to be the Impostor Expert on your own team or maybe find a therapist with this expertise. The Impostor Expert serves to keep you accountable to your recovery from your impostor triggers, symptoms, and behaviors. So, you may also be able to find this person by engaging with friends, family, and/or community members on the program in this book. This person serves as an accountability partner to help you to identify when you are struggling with impostor syndrome and to find strategies that might be useful to address the situation. They need to understand impostor syndrome, how it may be operating for you, and how to combat it proactively. So, here's an example of how I [Lisa] use my impostor experts to deal with my triggers:

> When I [Lisa] run into one of my impostor syndrome triggers, I immediately go to one of my impostor experts, who happen to be my partner, a couple of family members, and a close friend. They are really quick to point out the trigger and help me to get back on my feet to address the cognitive distortions. They check in with me after the trigger to assess where I am at and if I am using healthy, adaptive methods to address the issue and not going back to old patterns that reinforce my impostor syndrome.

Some people on your team will serve multiple roles, and others will only serve one. However, you must respect and value all members of your team because they all provide important and necessary social support that will be critical to your success at combating your impostor syndrome. It's important to recognize that a team needs to be cultivated. They don't just show up on your doorstep, ready to support your process. You have to look for them and, sometimes, assist them in being able to help you in the way that will be most productive for you.

Assess Your Dream Team Needs

In this exercise, name the people that can/do hold these roles for you. A person can hold more than one role, but it shouldn't be one person that holds all the roles. You should also assess where you need to fill the gaps.

DREAM TEAM ROLE	PERSON(S) WHO FILLS THE ROLE
The Mentor	
The Cheerleader	
The Grounder	
The Action Planner	
The Big-Picture Person	
The Impostor Expert	

• • •

SKILLS TO BUILD THE TEAM

TITRATING TRUST

When you are beginning the process of developing your team and trusting people with parts of your experience that you have rarely, if ever, shared, it's important to go slow. Whenever you are working to determine if someone belongs on your team, a strategic technique to use is Titrating Trust.

You typically first learn about titration in chemistry class, when you are adding chemicals to a solution. You learn to slowly drip the chemical into the solution and wait to see its impact. It is also a useful concept in interpersonal chemistry. In the very same way, you want to drip your trust in slow increments and see how the person responds. In the beginning, you share information that is of low threat, and as the person increasingly shows their trustworthiness, you can increase the level of sensitivity of the information.

As you share information with new people, reflect on some of these questions: Do you feel like the person honors your disclosure by listening and taking in the information? Do you sense that they are interested in how this impacts you? What kind of support do they provide? What roles might they fit on your dream team? Do you have any concerns about this person? Can you address these issues with the person?

CRAFTING FEEDBACK

When you think someone might be a great addition to your team but their feedback isn't always useful, you can help them to provide feedback that does become useful to your process. Sometimes, feedback can be too general to make an impact. For example, if after a difficult moment at work, you seek support from someone that you think could be a Grounder for you, and their response is something generic like, "You are going to be fine." While, in general, that is likely to be true, if you need more, you can follow the moment up with, "Do you use any techniques or tools to feel better when things feel out of sorts?" Feedback can also at times feel too harsh to be productive. In those cases, you can ask the person if they were able to see anything that you did positively. So, they can more actively "sandwich" the constructive feedback with positive feedback.

The key piece to observe here is that just because someone struggles to give you exactly what you need doesn't mean that they will always struggle. Just as you want to be very strong at receiving feedback, you also want your Dream Team to be solid at receiving feedback and responsive to how they can be more helpful to you.

ADDRESSING RUPTURES

In the course of a long, enduring relationship, ruptures occur—moments when there are disagreements, miscommunications, and disappointments. This is the natural course of relationships and learning how to address these ruptures and recover from them is important to having a team that is with you over the long haul. The benefits of a long-term Dream Team is that you have history. These team members will be with you over difficult moments that can come to a positive resolution through their support.

Commit to some key interpersonal skills to build a strong team. The first is open, transparent, but kind and relationship-sustaining, communication. Practice engaging with your team in an honest and direct way, never passive-aggressively. Aim not to hurt others, even accidentally. As immediately as possible, address any difficulties that occur between you and any member of your team. Commit to raising issues in a nondefensive way by using "I statements" and listening and paraphrasing what you hear when the person responds to you. Address any feedback about the relationship that you are given. For example, if someone on your team tells you that they find that you are relying on them too much, this could really trigger you. It could leave you thinking, "This is why I don't rely on other people." Try to remain nonreactive and realize when someone gives you constructive feedback, it's an act of intimacy and they want you to grow individually and in the relationship. So, don't run away from them. Appreciate the feedback from them, and then make sure that you get some details about recent experiences that have been problematic for them, so that you understand exactly what they are referencing. Then, you can make some changes in the way that you utilize them that correspond with the feedback. After some time, you can revisit this issue with them and ask them if the adjustments that you have made feel better to them.

Your Dream Team is valuable and you want to treat them as such. Do all the hard and worthwhile things in a relationship that allow you to maintain and grow these relationships. On the other side of the equation, if you start to realize that a team member cannot do the same, and is unable to do the hard work with you, consider replacing them for someone who may be a better fit from a growth perspective.

SUPPORTING OTHERS: PRACTICING THE ROLES

As we mentioned earlier, we are true believers in reciprocity in relationships. So, it's important that you are always trying to bring value back to the relationship by offering what you can in return. It's very powerful when you also serve as a Dream Team member for members of your own team. In addition, you can consider holding these supportive roles for other people in your life struggling with impostor syndrome. Taking up these roles can help you to develop empathy for those on your Dream Team, as it's not always easy to support someone struggling with impostor syndrome. It can bring a nuanced understanding to what you need from others, and how to support someone else with impostor syndrome with care.

As you finish Step 8, we want you to proactively craft your impostor syndrome dream team that will be there with you as you make new choices toward owning and living in your greatness. This step can take some time, but this does not mean you want to ignore it or minimize your efforts here. Your Dream Team is going to be invaluable to your changes and accountability to new behaviors. They are going to be the crew that will really understand where you have come from and how much there is to celebrate when you hit new milestones in your recovery from impostor syndrome.

IDENTIFY DREAM TEAM MEMBERS

My Dream Team

NAME	ROLE	WHEN TO REACH OUT

Identify the roles you currently need for your Dream Team and the person who might be able to fill it.

Roles To Fill

ROLE TYPE	POTENTIAL CANDIDATES	ACTIONS

ROLE TYPE	POTENTIAL CANDIDATES	ACTIONS

_____
_____
_____
_____
_____
_____
_____
_____

KEY TAKEAWAYS

- You've learned that recovering from impostor syndrome takes a team.

- You will consider working with a therapist or a coach, and the implications of working with each.

- You know you need different types of people on your impostor syndrome dream team (the Mentor, the Cheerleader, the Grounder, the Action Planner, the Big-Picture Person, the Impostor Expert). All are important, but the Mentors are foundational.

- You've learned key things to consider when choosing mentors.

- You've committed to engaging in healthy interpersonal behaviors with your Dream Team so that they can be with you long term.

Chapter 10

STEP 9: UNDERSTAND AND CREATE THE CONDITIONS FOR YOUR OPTIMAL PERFORMANCE

Welcome to the final step! We are so proud of you! You have made it through Steps 1 through 8, and you have WORKED! You have learned about the origins of your impostor syndrome, identified your triggers, crafted a new narrative to tell your own story, been able to share your accomplishments, learned how to silence your ANTs, developed a self-care plan and habits to sustain it, considered new roles to take up, and begun to build your impostor syndrome Dream Team. Now, we are going to put it all together so all your hard work goes with you always.

Unfortunately, when you struggle with impostor syndrome, you tend to operate under sub-optimal conditions, which only increase it. Jocelyn felt isolated and ashamed, and thought overworking would get her through her impostor feelings, but they never truly dissipated. Instead, as she was promoted, they intensified and caused her a great amount of distress.

We helped Jocelyn develop a plan of action to optimize her self-care and diminish her impostor syndrome experiences. This plan involved engaging in self-care activities that she enjoyed, such as going to her spin class and getting monthly massages. It also included reaching out to her team of mentors and supporters at least twice a month to discuss her impostor syndrome experiences and to seek assistance on how to address them.

When we work with clients in therapy or in coaching, a lot of change, and learning goes on over the course of the work. When a client finally "graduates" from the work (in clinical terms, this is usually referred to as "termination," but we think that has an ominous, dark sound to it that doesn't quite capture what is happening), it's a celebratory moment. Together, we have moved the needle on aspects of clients' lives that have felt impossible for them to change. Sometimes they have been generationally stuck, and we have created new ways of being that give the client new possibilities, options, freedom, and, hopefully, a renewed sense of hope. When the work is ending, often the clients are worried that they may not be able to continue succeeding in these ways without the therapist or the coach. They are worried that they haven't internalized us or the work. By this time, they usually have and there is plenty of evidence of it. However, to help them concretize all that they have learned, and to maintain the confidence they have gained through our work together, we have them develop "coping cards," a toolbox of all the important skills that they have learned throughout the work. Coping cards are a physical manifestation of all they have done and worked hard to master. Over the years, we have heard they are incredibly useful to have when they are feeling depleted and are triggered, and need a reminder of what to do in that moment. We have had clients who carry their coping cards in their wallets or purses at all times, and we have had some who develop them and never feel the need for them because the process was enough to remind them that "I got this."

So, let's develop your impostor syndrome toolbox of coping cards, which will serve as your individualized action plan to defeat impostor syndrome. In each section, we will have a card that you can cut out and laminate, or you can buy a set of index cards and write out the activity on the cards of your choice. If you decide that you would like to develop the cards in a digital format (e.g., on your phone or a Word document), please complete the cards in the book by hand before you transcribe them to that format. As you may remember from Step 2, handwriting allows you to process emotions in a deeper, more productive way.

It's important to do the last step because it is meant to help you internalize the work that you have just done and be able to take it with you into your life every day. We hope that the book and the first 8 steps have served as a powerful foundation for you to own your greatness, and to overcome impostor syndrome. We believe that your individual action plan, in the form of your coping cards, will enable you to sustain all that you have learned throughout the book, in order to minimize your impostor syndrome, and to live your best life.

CARD 1: THE ORIGIN AND NEW BEGINNINGS CARD

In Step 1, you explored in great detail the origins of your impostor syndrome. This helped to give you an understanding of some of your triggers. In a few lines, write out the most important factors that developed the impostor syndrome for you and how this has impacted how you think about certain dynamics in your family, around competition, and in regard to feedback. Then, list out some of the lessons that you learned about how you will move forward in regard to those dynamics.

For example, the dynamics that prompted my impostor syndrome were: "Being seen as the child who works hard, but is not naturally smart. I have a high need to please others. Achievement was always the way that I got seen."

The things that I learned from this are: "Do not compare my children against each other—they are each unique and bring their own skills and talents to what they do. It's okay not to always please other people, actually it's good for me not to; I can recognize myself for things other than my achievements, like being a kind and loving person, being good to myself, and staying present."

Origin and New Beginnings Card

THE DYNAMICS THAT PROMPTED MY IMPOSTOR SYNDROME WERE:

THE THINGS THAT I LEARNED FROM THIS ARE:

CARD 2: THE NEUTRALIZING TRIGGERS CARD

In Step 2, you identified your triggers and were specific about the people, places, and things that trigger your impostor syndrome, and you even directly confronted the feelings related to those experiences. In this card, you are going to identify your top triggers, your old response to those triggers, and your new, healthy, nonreactive positive response. The reason that you want to identify your old responses is because it will help you to notice them when they occur and to make other conscious and purposeful choices instead.

Here's an example of how to complete this card:

My trigger is "making mistakes, especially when they impact other people."

My old response is "Catastrophizing, feeling like I am bad, irresponsible, and incompetent, and ruminating about the mistake, constantly running through other choices that I should have made."

My new response is "saying and believing that all people make mistakes; realizing that I did not intentionally try to do a bad thing; grounding myself to get perspective on the actual impact of the mistake; and make a plan for the way that I will respond to the mistake in a manner that is appropriate to the situation."

The Neutralizing Triggers Card

TRIGGER	OLD RESPONSE	NEW RESPONSE

CARD 3: YOUR NEW NARRATIVE CARD

In Step 3, you worked on your new narrative so that you reframed your experience in ways that allow you to stand in your greatness. In this card, you are going to remember the thin aspects of your narrative and highlight the thickened pieces that you focused on in this step of your process. This card will be used when you feel yourself slipping into old, simple narratives of yourself that don't take in the deeper picture of you.

Here's an example of how you will complete this card:

My old thin narrative is: "I am not naturally smart—I know how to work hard."

My new thickened narrative is: "I have natural talents in so many things, and some things do come easier to me, like writing, interpersonal relationships, and coming up with creative solutions to problems and, yet, even these things require effort. There are things that I have to work on that I am also skilled at and have become my strengths, like mathematics, finance, and business. I do not need to overwork in order to prove my competence."

My New Narrative Card

OLD THIN NARRATIVE	NEW THICK NARRATIVE

CARD 4: SPEAK YOUR TRUTH AND KNOW YOUR STRENGTHS

In Step 4, you dug into your experience, were able to share your triggers with trusted people around you and to catalog your strengths. In this card, you are going to list every single strength, competence, and skill that you have and can own or are even working on owning.

List as many of your strengths as you can. If you have more than space allows on the card in the book, keep adding on a separate piece of paper or index card. You should have some already from Step 4 and also from the "IDENTIFY THREE OF YOUR STRENGTHS" activity in Step 2, but you are going to add more. When you are feeling that you are de-skilled and that you don't have any talents, this will remind you that you have many. You can refer back to Gardner's Multiple Intelligences chart in Step 4 to add more detail. But you should also consider strengths outside those multiple intelligences, including practical skills like cooking, cleaning, and organizing; socioemotional skills like assertiveness, humor, and patience; and leadership and business skills like negotiation, marketing, strategy, decision-making, and team building. Be expansive as you consider your repertoire of strengths.

Your Repertoire of Strengths Card

CARD 5: MOST POPULAR ANTs AND YOUR REPELLENT

In Step 5, you learned about Automatic Negative Thoughts (ANTs), which are common responses to triggers, and how to combat them with rational responses, your repellent to these nasty little critters that can be creepy, crawly thought monsters that affect how you feel and what you do.

In this card, we want you to list your most common ANTs, your trigger or category of triggers (e.g., receiving negative feedback), your old typical thoughts related to the ANTs, and your new, planned rational responses (positive statements and questions). For example, if one of the most common ANTs that you experience is Fortune-telling and the trigger that tends to elicit this ANT is risk-taking, your old response might be, "I am not going to take the lead on this project because if something goes wrong, I might lose my job." Your new rational response might be, "I am going to take the lead on this project. I can't predict what's going to happen, but I do know that I am a good project manager, have expertise in this area, and am excited about what this project could mean to my team and my career."

Most Popular ANTs and My Repellent Card

ANT TYPE	TRIGGER	OLD RESPONSE	RATIONAL RESPONSE

I practice my positive statement _____

(when) and _____ (where and with whom).

CARD 6: SELF-CARE COMMITMENTS

In Step 6, you discovered that poor self-care habits are a hallmark of people who have impostor syndrome. You learned how to value self-care and make it a nonnegotiable part of your life. On this card, list your commitments to your self-care, including your new self-care habits that you are going to commit to by time blocking them into your calendar and constantly making them visible. You will also have an opportunity to write out your commitment to frequency and make any kind of comments in the notes section that will enhance your commitment to the practice. For example, your self-care habit might be "Meditation" and in the notes section, you could add, "Ultimate goal is daily, but be kind to myself and start slow. Commit to one minute of meditation a day until I have successfully completed it for five days straight. Then add a minute every day I am successful, for five days." This allows you to set your ultimate goal as well as develop a plan to get started that is reasonable, kind, and focused on success.

Self-Care Commitments Card

SELF-CARE PRACTICE	NOTES

CARD 7: NEW ROLES

Step 7 helped clarify the roles that are typical for those with impostor syndrome, and how defeating the impostor syndrome means experimenting with new and unfamiliar roles. On this card, list the new roles you will be trying and in what situations they will be particularly relevant. If one of the new roles you will be trying on is Help-Seeker, then you should identify what old role you are replacing (e.g., "Knowledge Giver") and where this will be particularly important for you to be conscious (e.g., with siblings, on my team at work). The point of this card is to challenge yourself when in these situations to avoid typical roles and to look for opportunities to try new ways of being.

New Roles Card

THE NEW ROLE	THE OLD ROLE	RELEVANT SITUATION(S)

CARD 8: YOUR DREAM TEAM

In Step 8, you thought very critically about your support network and constructed a Dream Team to help you implement your new behavioral changes; to appreciate and assist you with slowing down and trying something new rather than something familiar that reinforces the impostor syndrome; and to guide and go along with you as you experience new places in your life, relationship, career, and within yourself that you never thought possible. Here, you are going to complete two cards. For the first card, create a reminder of who to go to and when. For the other card, identify which roles are missing, a possible individual who might fill this role, and what action you need to take. For the first card, it could look like: "When I feel down about a mistake, error, difficult moment, or risk has gone wrong, I will call Iman, my Cheerleader." The second card could look like: "For a potential Mentor, I will reconnect with Tangela, a former supervisor, on LinkedIn."

Your Dream Team Card

NAME	ROLE	WHEN TO REACH OUT

Roles to Fill Card

ROLE TYPE	POTENTIAL CANDIDATES	ACTIONS

CARD 9: YOUR KEY TAKEAWAYS

For the final card(s), you should add any additional learnings you had that you want to hold onto from engaging the book that were not included in the previous cards. For example, you might have found the cultural significance piece around people of color to have been particularly relevant to your experience. So, your Card 9 might have a reminder like, "Build more relationships with people who share my cultural experience," or "attend at least one cultural event per month." You might have had an epiphany about your family of origin that you want to keep front and center when you engage with them. Your card might say, "When visiting my parents, set boundaries around caretaking." Take the time to reflect on any other important experiences of learning that you had over the course of the book that you want to make sure that you carry away with you. Look at your margin notes or anything that you have highlighted that you need to hold onto moving forward. Create as many additional cards as you want.

Additional Key Takeaways

YOUR IMPOSTOR SYNDROME COPING CARD TOOLBOX

Creating your toolbox helps you to retain the learning and is your personalized action plan. The coping cards are a reminder of what learning you need to hold in the forefront of your mind until it's internalized. At times, you may need to carry them around, pull them out to take a step back and remind yourself of how to respond in a way that does not promote your impostor syndrome. In other words, your coping cards can and should be revisited and revised. They shouldn't stay static. As you learn something new or have a greater understanding of a situation, change the card to reflect that. After a time, when you review them, you'll notice yourself automatically engaging certain cards, meaning you've adopted the new behaviors. You can then put those cards aside.

Internalizing the work that you have done here will take some time, but before you realize it, some of the new skills will be second nature and the old habits will feel far away. But it takes practice. So, practice, practice, practice until you don't need to practice anymore because it is with you.

Chapter 11

OWN YOUR GREATNESS

This chapter will discuss how to own your greatness and keep your impostor syndrome at bay. It will review the steps of the 3 C's strategy explored throughout the book and conclude with the development of an impostor syndrome commitment statement. The case of Daniel illustrates how crucial it is to commit to owning your greatness in the face of constant challenges:

Daniel was a VP of finance for a small tech startup. He sought coaching to adjust to his new leadership role and to address his impostor syndrome, which impacted his confidence. Using the 3 C's strategy, Daniel was able to overcome his impostor syndrome and to gain the confidence he needed to excel in his role. In a brief period of time, as the company grew, he was promoted twice to his current role as VP of finance. He reported that his life as a whole improved, and during this period, he also got married and currently has a six-month-old daughter. Daniel returned to coaching because of the current upheaval at his job. His company was recently acquired by a larger firm, and although he was promoted to SVP as a result, Daniel began to experience intense impostor feelings during the first week in his new role, including intrusive thoughts about his lack of competence and his identity as a fraud. "I thought I was over my impostor syndrome, but it feels like it has roared back." During this phase of coaching, Daniel revisited some of the key steps of the 3 C's strategy, some which had fallen by the wayside. He was able to re-engage them and once again diminish the effects of his impostor syndrome.

During an interview, former First Lady Michelle Obama stated, "I still have impostor syndrome. It never goes away." She is pointing to a critical thing to understand about your work with impostor syndrome. The intention of this book is to severely diminish the power of impostor syndrome on your daily life and to help you come to terms with your greatness. Your goal should be to manage it to the point where generally it's contained and not the predominant way you interact with your world. We want to weaken its hold on you, develop your self-confidence, and help you to see how much power you have in your life.

The 3 C's (Clarify, Choose, and Create) Strategy is your toolkit to manage impostor syndrome, especially during periods when it may flare up. The more skilled you become with using the steps in the 3 C's program, the more capable you will be to neutralize impostor syndrome, to own your greatness, and to live your best life.

UNDERSTANDING LAPSE VS. RELAPSE

When we discuss how to overcome impostor syndrome, we generally identify it as a recovery process. You are trying to change your response to the stimuli, which may have increased your impostor feelings. The goal is that the triggers in the past, such as taking on a new job, working with a different team, or meeting new people will no longer have the same negative and powerful effect on you (e.g., constantly doubting your abilities, avoiding engagement, overworking). When you have reached a point in overcoming your impostor syndrome where your confidence is strengthened, you are optimistic about your abilities to handle obstacles, you have a good social support network, and you continue to seek growth opportunities for yourself, you are in recovery. However, this does not indicate that impostor feelings are gone forever. There may be times when they may return, and your response to them will demonstrate the difference between a lapse and a relapse.

A lapse is a momentary and minor setback, such as having some brief doubts about being able to handle a promotion but moving forward and accepting the opportunity. A relapse is a major and protracted hindrance to your success, such as overworking for months when you land a new job, fearing that unless you can prove your competence, you will soon be fired. When you experience a lapse, you want to go back to your toolbox of coping cards or reread a relevant chapter. You will encounter more lapses than relapses in your experiences. The expectation is that while the impostor syndrome is not totally eliminated, it becomes a much more minor factor in how you live your life and make key decisions, both professionally or personally.

Daniel returned to coaching because he needed support in understanding that what he was experiencing was more of a lapse than a relapse. He immediately became aware that he was in the presence of one of his triggers (e.g., a new role), began to employ some of his most effective self-care strategies (meditating, running, etc.), and constantly countered his automatic negative thoughts with more positive affirmations and rational responding. Although we had discussed the notion of lapse versus relapse during our previous coaching engagement, he had yet to experience it. Since it had been so long since a major trigger, Daniel became concerned that his impostor syndrome was back to stay. Once we revisited the conversation about the lapse versus relapse distinction, Daniel felt relieved and was able to neutralize his impostor feelings. He no longer felt the need to overwork, and upon further exploration, Daniel was able to engage his healthy coping strategies fairly easily again. He recognized that he was not practicing them on a regular basis because he was so confident and comfortable. So, when things became emergent again, he felt at a loss.

We also uncovered that Daniel was not in consistent contact with his Dream Team of mentors and advisors, who would have reinforced his more positive narrative and supported his healthy coping strategies. We then worked to create a new action plan to combat his impostor syndrome. Daniel was able to conclude our coaching work feeling well equipped to manage his impostor feelings and to diminish the power of his impostor syndrome on his daily life.

After reading this book and implementing the 3 C's Strategy to conquer your impostor syndrome, you may have a similar experience to Daniel's. That is, at some point, you may feel that you have completely wiped out your impostor syndrome, only to suffer a lapse when a major trigger reappears. With the 3 C's Strategy as part of your daily routine and practice, when your triggers emerge, which they most certainly will, you will feel fully prepared to neutralize any impostor feelings and prevent your impostor syndrome from interfering with your professional and personal lives. You will be able to continue to own your greatness, despite these triggers.

IDENTIFYING LAPSE VS. RELAPSE

Now that you understand the difference between a lapse and a relapse, describe an example of how a lapse would look in your life (e.g., not countering automatic negative thoughts for a few days, reverting to old roles for a day or two) versus how a relapse might manifest in your life (e.g., overworking for months, neglecting self-care for weeks, etc.)

_____

_____

_____

•••

BARRIERS TO CONSISTENTLY UTILIZING THE 3 C's STRATEGY

In a perfect world, you would be able to utilize the 3 C's Strategy and set it on autopilot forever. Since we don't live in a perfect world, the goal is for the 3 C's Strategy to become part of your daily habits and routine, and you must constantly nurture them. We also realize that there are possible barriers, which may make it more difficult to do so. Here's how to overcome the following barriers, in order for the 3 C's to stay front and center in your everyday practice.

SURVIVOR'S GUILT

When you conquer your impostor syndrome, you will feel much more optimistic about your life and your career, which may impact your relationships with family, friends, and colleagues, who may not yet have reached this point in their lives. They may have yet to overcome their impostor syndrome or may feel less optimistic for other reasons. Therefore, while you are celebrating your victory, it may be evident to you that other important people in your life are still struggling. As result, you may experience survivor's guilt and might feel a pull to let your impostor syndrome regain its strength in order to commiserate about work and personal challenges, or to engage in unhealthy habits with your friends, family members, and colleagues. In this context, survivor's guilt refers to the feelings of guilt you may have for moving forward in your life and career, when significant others in your life may still feel stuck. This example of Kenya explores the difficulty of managing survivor's guilt and the importance of doing so:

Kenya is a marketing manager who sought coaching to manage her impostor syndrome because she felt consistently marginalized at her organization, and wanted to explore how to navigate this environment while also thinking about other career options. As a result of our work together, Kenya decided to pursue and eventually accept a role in development for a nonprofit women's rights organization. While Kenya was overjoyed by this outcome, she was a bit troubled by an unexpected result of it. She began to notice that some of her family members and friends, with whom she used to share career challenges since they were also in difficult work environments, no longer talked about their jobs with her. "Oh, you don't understand anymore, now that you are so happy," some of them would chide her when she asked about their work. Kenya started to feel a sense of distance developing between her and them, and she became saddened and guilty about it. She raised this concern in one of our coaching sessions. Kenya recognized that she had made it through a very painful time by utilizing the 3 C's Strategy, and she was grateful for the outcome. However, she realized that through the process, it felt like she had left some people behind. Kenya thought she was undeserving of it. Her intention was not to distance herself from her loved ones, but to conquer her impostor syndrome. Unfortunately, her success in defeating her impostor syndrome changed the dynamic of some of her relationships. Rather than allow the impostor syndrome to return to power to connect with them, the solution to managing her survivor's guilt was to process this experience with her friends and family members, and to provide support to them in any way she possibly could to help them to think about more optimistic possibilities. She sometimes served as their impostor expert, as they were open to having her support them in this way. After having these conversations with them, which were very productive, Kenya felt newly empowered to continue enjoying her success, while still connecting with her friends, but in a new way.

Managing Survivor's Guilt

You may have the same concerns and feelings as Kenya, and the key to addressing them is to first be able to identify them as survivor's guilt. Then you may wish to process these feelings with members of your Dream Team, and to explore how to communicate it to those individuals who may still be struggling and with whom you may sense a growing distance. Adopting an abundance mentality (where you acknowledge that everyone can succeed) will enable you to see that rather than being miserable together, you and all your loved ones deserve to conquer impostor syndrome and live a great life. There is room for everyone to do so.

MAJOR LIFE CHANGES OR DISRUPTIONS

As you may already know, life doesn't always go as scripted. Your five-year plan may suddenly derail or go off in another direction. When major life changes or disruptions (e.g., sudden job loss, relationship breakup, even positive disruptions, etc.) occur, it is very easy to let the 3 C's Strategy fall to the bottom of your priority list. If you are dealing with an unforeseen event, it is expected that you might lose focus. When such a situation occurs, rely on your self-care and tap into your Dream Team for social support to ensure that your impostor syndrome does not gain control of your functioning during this period.

SUMMARY OF THE 3 C's STRATEGY

As we conclude, it is important to revisit the strategy to clearly outline the process of owning your greatness, beating self-doubt, and overcoming impostor syndrome.

PHASE 1: CLARIFY (STEPS 1 TO 3)

In the Clarify phase, you gained insight into your impostor syndrome origin story and how it impacted your functioning (Step 1). You were able to identify your triggers and how to respond to them (Step 2), and changed your narrative to a more positive, thickened one (Step 3).

PHASE 2: CHOOSE (STEPS 4 TO 6)

In the Choose phase, you learned how to speak your truth, including owning your strengths and accomplishments (Step 4). You developed awareness and skills to silence your automatic negative thoughts (Step 5) and you learned how to value yourself by prioritizing your self-care (Step 6).

PHASE 3: CREATE (STEPS 7 TO 9)

In the final phase, Create, you began to experiment with new roles (Step 7), began the steps to build an impostor syndrome Dream Team of supporters and mentors (Step 8), and create your individualized action plan of coping cards (Step 9) that you can take with you as you internalize all the steps, and to recognize the optimal conditions for your success.

KEY TAKEAWAYS

- You recognize the difference between a lapse and a relapse in overcoming impostor syndrome.

- You identified some typical barriers to owning your greatness, such as survivor's guilt and major life disruptions, and how to manage them.

- You revisited the 3 C's Strategy to reinforce each step for your own clarity.

CONCLUSION

The journey to conquering impostor syndrome begins with your commitment to valuing yourself and choosing a different path for your life. You have made the decision to no longer be silenced or marginalized due to your impostor syndrome. You have taken the power into your own hands to alter the trajectory of your life. There will be points along the path where you will hit roadblocks, and that is when you will use your coping cards and reach out to your Dream Team. When your confidence wanes, remember that you have the knowledge and skills to meet the challenges before you. Impostor syndrome can be defeated, and the 3 C's Strategy is your roadmap to do so, in a clear and methodical way. This is the beginning of an exciting phase in your life, where reaching goals will not be met by feeling helpless to impostor feelings that may arise.

We are thrilled that you have taken these steps by arriving at this stage of the book. Owning your greatness, beating self-doubt, and overcoming impostor syndrome entail commitment, effort, and insight. With the tools of the 3 C's Strategy, we are confident that you will be able to reach your goals and live the great life you dreamed of, unencumbered by impostor syndrome, free to realize your optimal self, and able to recognize that it is a continuous but wonderful journey, one that can be guided by your support network and your resolve to honor yourself.

YOUR IMPOSTOR SYNDROME COMMITMENT

Write a commitment statement about how you will deal with obstacles as they come up to avoid relapse. After you complete it, read it aloud to yourself.

_____

_____

_____

_____

BIBLIOGRAPHY

Barbara Cromwell, Nina W. Brown, Janice Sanchez-Huceles, and Fred L. Adair, "The Impostor Phenomenon and Personality Characteristics of High School Honor Students," *Journal of Social Behavior and Personality* 5, no. 6 (1990): 563–73.

Carol S. Dweck, *Mindset: The New Psychology of Success* (New York: Random House, 2006).

Catherine Cozzarelli and Brenda Major, "Exploring the Validity of the Impostor Phenomenon," *Journal of Social and Clinical Psychology* 9, no. 4, (1990): 401–17.

Claude M. Steele and Joshua Aronson, "Stereotype Threat and the Intellectual Test Performance of African Americans," *Journal of Personality and Social Psychology* 69, no. 5 (1995): 797–811.

Diana P. Dudau, "The Relation between Perfectionism and Impostor Phenomenon," *Procedia—Social and Behavioral Sciences* 127 (2014): 129–33.

D. L. Bernard, L. S. Hoggard, and E. W. Neblett, Jr., "Racial Discrimination, Racial Identity, and Impostor Phenomenon: A Profile Approach," *Cultural Diversity and Ethnic Minority Psychology* 24, no. 1 (2018): 51–61.

Howard Gardner, *Frames of Mind: The Theory of Multiple Intelligences* (New York: Basic Books, 1983).

Jasmine Vergauwe, Bart Wille, Marjolein Feys, Filip De Fruyt, Frederik Anseel, "Fear of Being Exposed: The Trait-Relatedness of the Impostor Phenomenon and Its Relevance in the Work Context," *Journal of Business and Psychology* 30, no. 3 (2015): 565–81.

John Gravois, "You're Not Fooling Anyone," in *If I'm So Successful, Why Do I Feel Like a Fake?* eds. Joan C. Harvey and Cynthia Katz (New York: Random House, 1985).

Julie E. King and Eileen L. Cooley, "Achievement Orientation and the Impostor Phenomenon among College Students," *Contemporary Educational Psychology* 20, no. 3 (1995): 304–12.

Karen W. Tao and Alberta M. Gloria, "Should I Stay or Should I Go? The Role of Impostorism in STEM Persistence," *Psychology of Women Quarterly* 43, no. 2 (2018): 1–14.

Kevin Cokley, Germine H. Awad, Leann Smith, Stacey Jackson, Olufunke Awosogba, Ashley Hurst, Steven Stone-Sabali, Lauren Blondeau, and Davia Roberts, "The Roles of Gender Stigma Consciousness, Impostor Phenomenon, and Academic Self-Concept in the Academic Outcomes of Women and Men," *Sex Roles* 73, no. 9 (2015): 414–26.

Kevin Cokley, Shannon McClain, Alicia Enciso, and Mercedes Martinez, "An Examination of the Impact of Minority Status Stress and Impostor Feelings on the Mental Health of Diverse Ethnic Minority College Students," *Journal of Multicultural Counseling and Development* 41, no. 2 (2013): 82–95.

Kris Henning, Sydney Ey, Darlene Shaw, "Perfectionism, the Impostor Phenomenon and Psychological Adjustment in Medical, Dental, Nursing and Pharmacy Students," *Medical Education*, 32, no. 5 (1998): 456–64.

Lauren A. Blondeau and Germine H. Awad, "The Relation of the Impostor Phenomenon to Future Intentions of Mathematics-Related School and Work," *Journal of Career Development* 45, no. 3 (2018): 253–67.

Lenora M. Yuen and Devora S. Depper, "Fear of Failure in Women," *Women & Therapy* 6, no. 3 (2010): 21–39.

Loretta N. McGregor, Damon E. Gee, and Elizabeth K. Posey, "I Feel Like a Fraud and It Depresses Me: The Relation Between the Impostor Phenomenon and Depression," Social Behavior and Personality 36, no. 1 (2008): 43–48.

Marie-Hélène Chayer and Thérèse Bouffard, "Relations between Impostor Feelings and Upward and Downward Identification and Contrast among 10- to 12-Year-Old Students," *European Journal of Psychological Education* 25, no. 1 (2010): 125–40.

Monica McGoldrick, Randy Gerson, and Sueli Petry, *Genograms: Assessment and Intervention*, 3rd ed. (New York: W.W. Norton & Company, 2008).

M. Neureiter and E. Traut-Mattausch, "An Inner Barrier to Career Development: Preconditions of the Impostor Phenomenon and Consequences for Career Development," *Frontiers in Psychology* 4, no. 48 (2016): 37–48.

Nell Gluckman, "How a Dean Got Over Impostor Syndrome — and Thinks You Can, Too," *The Chronicle of Higher Education*, December 1, 2017 issue.

Pauline R. Clance and Suzanne A. Imes, "The Impostor Phenomenon in High-Achieving Women: Dynamics and Therapeutic Interventions," *Psychotherapy: Theory, Research, and Practice* 15, no. 3 (1978): 241–47.

Rebecca L. Badawy, Brooke A. Gazdag, Jeffrey R. Bentley, and Robyn L. Brouer, "Are All Impostors Created Equal? Exploring Gender Differences in the Impostor Phenomenon-Performance Link," *Personality and Individual Differences* 131, no. 1 (2018): 156–63.

Richard P. Brown and Patricia L. Gerbarg, *The Healing Power of the Breath* (Boston: Shambhala Publications, Inc., 2012).

Richard G. Gardner, Jeffrey S. Bednar, Bryan W. Stewart, James B. Oldroyd, Joseph Moore, "'I Must Have Slipped through the Cracks Somehow': An Examination of Coping with Perceived Impostorism and the Role of Social Support," *Journal of Vocational Behavior* 115 (2019).

Robert L. Leahy, Stephen J. F. Holland, and Lata K. McGinn, *Treatment Plans and Interventions for Depression and Anxiety Disorders* (New York: Guilford Press, 2011).

Shamala Kumar and Carolyn M. Jagacinski, "Imposters Have Goals Too: The Imposter Phenomenon and Its Relationship to Achievement Goal Theory," *Personality and Individual Differences* 40, no. 1 (2006): 147–57.

Staffan Noteberg, *Pomodoro Technique Illustrated: The Easy Way to Do More in Less Time* (Dallas, Texas: Pragmatic Bookshelf, 2010).

Stephen J. Dollinger and Nerella V. Ramainiah, "Applying the Big Five Personality Factors to the Impostor Phenomenon," *Journal of Personality Assessment* 78, no. 2 (2002): 321–33.

ACKNOWLEDGMENTS

We would like to take a moment to enthusiastically express our appreciation to the Ulysses Press staff for their support in making this book possible, especially Bridget Thoreson (thank you for that special call that started this amazing process and all your cheerful, kind, patient, and supportive encouragement) and Ashten Evans (thank you for your editorial feedback) and Renee Rutledge (thank you for your deep editorial guidance).

We are forever grateful to our clients who have chosen us as their partners in their collaborative growth journey. We are honored that you allow us or have allowed us to support your goals and be a safe place for your emotional vulnerability. We are proud of all the ways you challenge yourselves to reach for your dreams. You motivate us to be ever better and also appreciate our authentic selves in the work simultaneously.

We would like to thank our daughters, Nia and Maya, for their patience, love, and unwavering support as we worked on the manuscript for countless weekends and nights. Your cheerful encouragement and ebullient anticipation enabled us to fully immerse ourselves into the process of completing this book, and you inspire us every day to do our part in making the world a better and brighter place for you.

We would also like to thank all of our friends and families, especially our parents, Anna and Francisco Orbé, and Marguerite and Guy Austin, for inspiring us to always dream big, and to believe in the power of our abilities to make an impact on the world and in our lives. Thank you to our sisters for cheering us on and always helping us to be tapped into the excitement of the work!

Rich: I want to send a note of appreciation to my mentors Drs. Bob Fullilove, Mary McRae, Joseph Ponterotto, and Lisa Whitten, who each uniquely supported my journey to becoming a psychologist along different stages of my academic and career paths. I would like to express my eternal gratitude and to honor the memories of my Aunt Jeanette Lefevre and Mr. Richie Perez, who have influenced me to always engage with others through a spirit of love, humility, and a fervent commitment to justice and humanity.

Lisa: I want to thank my mentors, Drs. Vanessa Bing and Diane Ducat, for inspiring me to have the practice that I have. You allowed me to dream and create a professional life that I never thought possible. To my Titi Mayda, thank you for always sending special prayers and thoughts, and for having incredible belief in me. Thank you to Kiyan Fox for all of your design support and help with taking a concept and making it into an understandable image. Thanks to my PWF family for bringing community into our lives in ways I never thought possible. You have shown me Wakanda is real.

ABOUT THE AUTHORS

Dr. Lisa Orbé-Austin is a licensed psychologist and executive coach with a focus on career advancement, leadership development, and job transitions. She is a cofounder and partner of Dynamic Transitions Psychological Consulting, a career and executive coaching consultancy, where she works mostly with high-potential managers and executives. She earned her doctorate in counseling psychology from Columbia University. Her views about career advancement, job transitions, leadership, and diversity and inclusion are regularly sought by the media, and she has appeared in outlets such as *The New York Times*, *NBC News*, *Forbes*, *The Huffington Post*, *Refinery29*, *Business Insider*, and *Insight Into Diversity*.

Dr. Orbé-Austin has been an invited speaker at various national conferences and regularly consults to organizations in the private sector, non-profits, and educational institutions in supporting their employees and senior leadership teams to address gender bias, diversity, equity, and inclusion concerns, leadership development, effective communication, team cohesion, and conflict management. Her practice also consults to universities on the reorganization and evaluation of their career centers to enhance their efficacy and metrics, in order to improve service delivery, data analysis, and student career outcomes.

Richard Orbé-Austin, PhD, is a licensed psychologist, executive coach, and organizational consultant. He was the founding director of NYU's Graduate Student Career Development Center, developing the strategic vision and leading a team responsible for managing the career needs of over 14,000 master's and doctoral students in over 100 different disciplines. Prior to his tenure at NYU, Dr. Orbé-Austin served in a variety of leadership roles, including as the chief diversity officer at Baruch College—City University of New York and as president of the NY Association of Black Psychologists.

In his practice located in New York City, Dr. Orbé-Austin works with executives and high-potential managers to identify their best-fit career options, advance their career goals, and strengthen their leadership skills. He also regularly consults to academic institutions, corporations, and nonprofit organizations on issues related to diversity, equity and inclusion, higher education career services, career development and transitions, leadership, communication, and conflict. Dr. Orbé-Austin's opinions and writings have appeared in a variety of publications, including Forbes, Fast Company, HigherEdJobs.com, Career Convergence, Ebony.com, and Diversity Executive.